"If you are unemployed or you know someone who has suffered sudden job loss, then this book is a must-read. Helen offers you a realistic assessment of today's changing job market and practical advice to survive tough times.

"In addition, she provides spiritual guidance and help quite unlike a lot of other books that tackle this difficult subject.

"This book is jam-packed with valuable and up-to-date job search information."

Tom Sawyer, Outplacement Consultant,
Careers That Work,
San Mateo, California

"Helen is an encourager, and this book is full of encouragement. This is practical, down-to-earth, rubber-meets-the-road material. Anyone who is unemployed will benefit immensely from this book.

"The insights she provides reflect the Helen I know. I lived through her seventeen-month ordeal with her and can attest to her credibility and deep trust in God."

Barbara Johnson, author of *Stick a Geranium in Your Hat and Be Happy* and many others; founder of Spatula Ministries

**suddenly
unemployed**

suddenly unemployed

Encouraging & Practical Steps
for Finding a Job

HELEN KOOIMAN HOSIER

Revell

Grand Rapids, Michigan

Published by Fleming H. Revell
a division of Baker Publishing Group
P.O. Box 6287, Grand Rapids, MI 49516-6287

Previously published in 1992 under the title *Suddenly Unemployed: How to Survive Unemployment and Land a Better Job!* by Here's Life Publishers.

Printed in the United States of America

Library of Congress Cataloging-in-Publication Data
Hosier, Helen Kooiman.
    Suddenly unemployed : encouraging & practical steps for finding a job / Helen Kooiman Hosier.
        p.   cm.
    Originally published: San Bernardino, CA : Here's Life Publishers, c1992.
    Includes bibliographical references and index.
    ISBN 0-8007-5924-9 (pbk.)
    1. Job hunting—United States. 2. Career changes—United States. 3. Unemployment—Psychological aspects. I. Title.
HF5382.75.U6H67 2005
650.14—dc22   2004022808

Contents

Introduction

Suddenly Unemployed was born out of the crucible of a seventeen-month experience with an unexpected job loss that sent me reeling. That I survived is not a credit to my ingenuity, my smarts, networking, or any of one or a combination of many things I did to get through this ordeal. Although the things I learned from this experience were helpful, and I know they will work to your benefit, what really carried me through was reliance on my strong faith and understanding of God's almightiness. This, more than anything, I want to impart to you. Without God's help, I would have succumbed to discouragement and despair. That it took so long to become reemployed was not God's fault, as some may be tempted to say. I had a lot to learn, and I earned my degree in the school of hard knocks!

In sharing this experience, I can come alongside you, as it were, in what you are going through and encourage you to recognize that you are not in this alone and that you will get to the other side. God wants to be your helper, your comfort, and all the other things you need right now. He wants to do for you what you cannot do by yourself. God

9

is going to teach you some amazing things in this present crucible. He has a purpose, and your part is to trust him as your faith is enlarged.

Job loss is widespread; everything you read about, see on TV, or hear on the radio amplifies the enormity of this nationwide problem. Today's statistics may be obsolete next week, so you will not find a lot of statistical information in this book. You can find the latest updates nationwide and in your local area on the Internet. Go, for instance, to www.bls.gov for mind-boggling information (BLS stands for Bureau of Labor Statistics). Joblessness varies from one part of the country to the next; certain sections are hit harder than others. Much depends on the types of work performed in an area. Joblessness does not remain static.

In 1991 when I was suddenly unemployed, I recall talking to my friends Julie and Joe about the underreporting of the jobless in this country at that time. "Of course it varies from state to state, month by month," I said. "One study concludes that at least 19.6 million Americans are unemployed or underemployed, more than 14.7 million are jobless, and not quite another 4.9 million are working part-time when what they need is full time. That yields a real unemployment rate of 16.5 percent, which, according to some specialists, is still an undercount."

Joe responded that where his son lived, the August 1991 unemployment figure stood at 11 percent. I told him that nationwide the Bureau of Labor Statistics reports seemed highly inaccurate. "When I inquired of bureau officials about how the unemployment figures are reached," I said, "I was told on three different occasions by knowledgeable individuals in three different states that it is based on current filings for unemployment benefits." I explained that such statistics are inaccurate indicators. They do not include those whose unemployment benefits have run out or those who don't qualify for unemployment because their former employers are nonprofit and don't pay in. Homeless unemployed people probably are not counted. Such statistics also do not count welfare recipients, temps (who cannot be counted as fully employed), or others trying to eke out a living on so-called self-employment. I pointed these things out to my friends at that time, and I want you to pay attention as you read this, for it is just as true today as it was then.

To be unemployed is a very serious matter—if one were to try to factor in these things, the statistics would be staggering. The government's statistics are what some analysts call "a blatant lie," "fake," "chicanery," "fictionalized reporting," "doctored surveys," and "hollow rhetoric." It is highly probable that America now has the highest unemployment in the Western industrial world. The rhetoric of the government and politicians rings hollow. "They need to talk to the unemployed and their families," I said to my friends then. "That, of course, is the problem. Many of us knew *we* weren't counted." I told them that according to polls and research findings I had been following for a long time, the vast majority of people are profoundly affected by joblessness. I explained that, for instance, more than 58 percent of those surveyed for a *New York Times/CBS News* poll said they knew someone well who was out of work.

Julie looked at me as I was relating all this and said, "Hmm, if they had polled us, we wouldn't have responded that way. We don't know anyone who is unemployed, do we, Joe?"

"Julie!" I said. "What do you mean? You're looking at one. I'm unemployed."

She was silent for a moment. "Oh!" she gasped. "I don't think of you that way. I mean, you don't look unemployed, and you don't talk like you're unemployed."

"Well, thank you," I said. "I'll take that as a compliment. But the truth is, I am without a job. In fact, I have been for a long time."

Meet the Unemployed

That conversation occurred many years ago, but you can see that things haven't changed that much. Compare those statements and the present state of affairs, and you immediately realize that job loss is nothing new. But when it strikes you—regardless if it is your first such experience or one of those déjà vu experiences—it is never painless.

In this book, you will discover who the unemployed are and how they feel. You may be surprised at how they look. Quite possibly you will meet yourself.

When I lost my job, I asked myself, "How can I enlist the pain of job loss to work for me, not against me?" Perhaps you are wondering if that is possible.

How do you go through job loss without experiencing undue trauma? Can the bad be minimized? Can any good come out of something so distressing? Can the good be maximized?

According to Richard Bolles, who writes the popular *What Color Is Your Parachute?* books, in a personal conversation I had with him, 80 percent of the population of the United States believe in God, and they want to know how their faith relates to their job hunt or career change. This being true, those of us who hold to our religious beliefs know we have another dimension going that does work for our good. This doesn't mean we can adopt a do-nothing attitude. God doesn't bless laziness and an inappropriate use of Scriptures. But we can know that God has a plan for our lives, and this focus will keep us balanced.

Of course, all of the facts regarding being unemployed call for responsibility on our part—*response-ability*—the ability to choose one's response, as Stephen Covey defines it in his book *The Seven Habits of Highly Effective People*.[1]

We must accept the responsibility to do what I call the "near at hand things" to bring order and stability into our lives and to respond to the pain and emotions that rise within us, according to our internalized values. This calls for patience, faith, and trust. It means relying on biblical truths so that they, rather than human impulses, drive our thinking and decision making.

For some, this dimension of keeping your focus on God and trusting him is new. You may never have thought of your work as being related to your belief in God. Now, however, perhaps you find yourself desperately crying out for help. It is my sincere prayer that this book will help you not only in your job search but also in your understanding of how much God loves you and longs to help you.

Looking Ahead

Even though I don't know what the particular circumstances were that caused you to join the ranks of the unemployed, I want you to know that I understand and care. I too was deeply wounded by my job loss. I know how it hurts, how the pain of rejection can all but knock you off your feet, how anger can well up unbidden. I know about fear, anxiety, and financial concerns.

You are presently confronted with an enormous challenge—that of finding another position in a job market that is overrun with people in the same circumstances as you. Being jobless in a recessionary market is like being on a roller coaster—one moment your hopes are up, and the next they come crashing down. Even in good times, to be without a job when you depend on a paycheck is one of the most traumatic things that can happen to you.

I did a lot of research for this book. I stood in line at our local Department of Human Resources talking to those waiting to sign up for unemployment benefits. I asked questions of the homeless roaming the streets. I interviewed CEOs who had lost their jobs and individuals with long tenure who had been terminated and were in a state of shock. I contacted outplacement and career consultants for their advice. I spent countless hours researching on the Internet. And I read books and articles by experts in the field.

Along with all the good material I uncovered, you will find survival tactics to help you cope with the stresses of unemployment. I have provided practical insights and steps to take all along the way, as well as tips for bouncing back. Spiritual encouragement as your faith is being tested is essential. You will also find that in these pages. Everything in this book is intended to help you think about the direction your life is going during this transition period.

Those of us who have experienced job loss are among the "wounded soldiers of the marketplace," many of us victims of injustice. We may not look or talk like the unemployed—whatever that stereotype is supposed to be—but we are real people.

You will have days when you feel you have taken three steps forward but fallen two behind. Keeping your focus on God, where it belongs, will empower you on a daily basis, moment by moment, as you walk on in faith.

At the time of my job loss, God impressed on my mind these words:

> "For I know the plans I have for you," declares the LORD, "plans to prosper you and not to harm you, plans to give you hope and a future."
>
> Jeremiah 29:11 NIV

I give them to you at the outset of this book, trusting that they will be a lifeline for you.

Part 1

Where You Are Today

We shouldn't view loss of a job as a finished landscape. We all are in process of being. Where you are now is but a part of that process. Why you are there requires examination and evaluation. What you do next can be an exciting prospect.

1

When the Unthinkable Happens to You

It happens, and when it does, being fired seems like the end of the world.

The unthinkable has happened: you have lost your job. You are a part of a vast reconfiguration of the world of work. Are you frightened? Hurting? Angry? Struggling with a lot of feelings and emotions you don't understand? What now?

What Now?

Our immediate reaction to unemployment is one of shock, disbelief, panic—and questions. How will we pay our bills? They won't stop just because we're out of work. What are the odds that we'll find new employment before unemployment benefits run out? Perhaps you, like me, don't even qualify for unemployment because your former employer hasn't paid into it. Talk about a shock! But the psychological toll may

17

prove to be the most difficult of all. How do we handle the stigma associated with job loss?

Hopefully, this book will provide guidance as you search for answers. Because I have been where you are, I have already done a lot of searching. Quite possibly, what I have learned can spare you from making some mistakes and expending needless effort, time, and even money. Moreover, my aim is to provide reassurance that you are going to make it. (If you haven't read the introduction to this book, take the time to refer back to it now.)

What's Happening?

Let's get this thing in focus. What has happened to you and to millions of others is, for the most part, becoming increasingly commonplace nationwide. The American security blanket—a good long-term job—is falling apart. It has always been somewhat frayed around the edges, but now it appears to be unraveling in some surprising ways. In times past, blue-collar workers quickly found themselves out of jobs when hard times came, but now hardly anyone is exempt.

Dramatic shifts in employment trends are taking place, and this is having a profound effect on the nature of work and on the relationship between employers and employees. Insourcing and outsourcing, two words being tossed around a lot in the current employment and unemployment environment, are taking their toll on the American workforce. Salary stagnation is another ugly reality.

It's Not Your Fault

From every corner of the economy, alarm bells are going off. You can't pick up a newspaper or magazine without reading about changes taking place. What has happened to you is not an isolated incident. Very likely your present unemployment predicament is not your fault. Mergers, take-overs, and acquisitions have been increasing at a feverish pitch during the last several years, and human displacement can be seen all around. Moreover, work going overseas as many companies outsource their work is leaving hundreds of thousands of workers suddenly unemployed. This is not just a trend; it is a new order with the tide of outsourcing rising.

Knowing that so many others have shared your fate may not provide much consolation. But I was able to look at my own job loss more objectively once I got a handle on what was taking place. You will need to do that too. As Richard Bolles says, rejection shock is real, and that, basically, is what job loss amounts to. "From our youth up, we are taught to hate rejection," he reminds us. "But then, along comes the job hunt. Eight times in our lifetime we have to go through this painful process. And, except at its very end, it is *nothing but* a process of rejection."[1]

Ambushed by a Pink Slip

One man wrote to a newspaper columnist explaining that because of the lack of employment opportunities in his region, he had resorted to cutting out articles on unemploy-ment just to remind himself that his current predicament wasn't his fault.

He went on to describe his circumstances—circumstances similar to those of many of the people with whom I have talked. He was a white-collar worker pursuing an MBA, but he found himself in the unemployment line every other Mon-day morning at 9:00 a.m. His corporate climb was halted by a layoff he never saw coming. He considered himself to have an acute perception of his environment and believed the best solution to any problem was to see it coming and take measures to prevent it from happening in the first place. But then he was ambushed by a pink slip. He did a wise thing: he began to question everything relative to his unemployment status, from his career choice to the area where he lived; and after analyzing his situation, he came to the conclusion that it wasn't his fault. As I looked at his predicament and saw how he felt betrayed by society, I fully empathized.

Where Are the Jobs?

I don't want to paint a doom and gloom picture for you. But I do want to portray the job situation accurately, not only so you can better understand what is taking place, but also so you can see that what you decide to do at this juncture in your life is very, very important. Once you understand the big picture, you can zero in on your own situation and maximize your efforts to reposition yourself in today's work culture.

American industry as a whole has seen a shift from goods-producing to service-providing employment. While this isn't a brand-new development, it still is not totally understood.

I first became aware of this shift when I worked as a technical writer in the quality control department of a world-famous toy designer and manufacturer. One morning our department was called together and told to clean up our computers, finish our work, and be prepared to vacate our offices by noon. Employees looked at each other in bewilderment—all 150 of them! And that was just one department. Before the "downsizing"—a heartless word for layoffs—was over, 45 percent of the people in that company were without work. It made the headlines in the *Wall Street Journal* and in business journals and newspapers across the country.

What happened there has become all too commonplace nationwide, with some industries being affected more than others. According to one Commerce Department study, the implementation of the North American Free Trade Agreement would lead to job losses of more than 40 percent in three dozen U.S. industries, including automobile parts, steel, shoes, and textiles. And why not? If you can get something made in a foreign country for $0.41 an hour (Turkey), $0.42 an hour (India), $1.22 an hour (Hungary), $1.50 an hour (Brazil), or $1.57 an hour (Mexico), in contrast to hourly wages for some jobs in this country, why shouldn't the work go overseas?[2]

At least that was the rationale behind what was projected to occur, and in the intervening years since that report was released, this is precisely what has happened. In fact, many companies have moved entire plants out of the country. That means job loss. We stand back, watch what is happening, and groan and moan as CEOs of these greedy mega-corporations continue to rake in their obscene salaries and bonuses while the little people in communities nationwide get badly hurt.

The Great Squeeze-Out

There are other explanations for the shift in the American job market, including legal and regulatory changes, scientific and technological advances, changes in consumer tastes and preferences, mechanization, and business organization and management changes. Factories, for instance, are replacing hands with machines that work 168 hours a week and don't go on strike.

Call it what you wish—some have suggested liberation; others say abandonment, a perestroika of sorts, or a savage new twist in the corporate struggle for existence. But this great squeeze-out is causing tremendous changes in the world of work. While it is creating new patterns of opportunity, risk is also involved, forcing us all into new ways of thinking.

Aggressive foreign rivals have forced many U.S. companies once looked upon as giants to cut back. A national television program reminded me that, as a nation, we have been importing more than we are exporting, and that a negative balance of trade always costs jobs. That is part of the big picture, and the effects filter down to the person on the street—you and me.

My own research of the job market revealed that service-providing industries are both the largest and the fastest-growing industries. In particular, health care will continue to be one of the most important groups of industries in terms of job creation as a growing and aging population increases the demand for health services. *The Occupational Outlook Handbook* (which will provide you with valuable information and can be seen on the Internet at www.bls. gov or studied at the library) affirms that some of the fastest-growing occupations are health related.

Perhaps you are thinking, *That's interesting, but I'm not a doctor, a nurse, or any other kind of health worker.* Service-providing industries include not only the health industry, but also finance, insurance, and real estate. Also available are government jobs; transportation, communications, and utilities positions; and wholesale and retail trade opportunities.

Business services are another large industry group accounting for ongoing growth and employment opportunities. Personnel supply services, which includes temporary help agencies, is the largest industry in this group.

"Why is that true?" you may ask. Consider the savings to industry and business. If certain services can be obtained through a temp agency, and the company doesn't have to pay for benefit packages (medical, retirement, and vacation), it makes fiscal sense to use temporaries. Temporary staffing is always among the first to note a rebound in market activity. Companies are very cautious when the market is unpredictable; consequently, they will turn to temporary help first rather than bring in an entire new workforce. Administrative and office workers tend to lag behind workers in labor-intensive fields in reemployment, and temp workers in construction, manufacturing, and other manual labor jobs benefit when there is a pickup in the economy. "You're going to put the person to work on the production floor—the guy who's actually boxing the widgets—before you hire the administrator," says Stacey Burke, Labor Ready spokesman.[3] (See chapter 2 for ideas on how temping can work for you.)

A New Era in the Work World

A rapidly increasing demand from business firms, government agencies, and privately owned businesses has opened the door for individuals with an entrepreneurial spirit. Bill collectors and plumbers, as diverse as their functions are, always seem to be in demand, and they offer legitimate business services. What unique business service do you have to offer? Many unemployed individuals have formed their own business or consulting services. Armed with their special portfolio of abilities, they have captured the attention of decision makers in businesses and are carving a niche for themselves. Almost every day people hang literature on my door advertising their services. I admire what they are doing and have often been able to use a person's services because he or she has taken this initiative.

The most venturesome way to work part-time is to sell your services as a freelancer or consultant. Some consultants rent out their services by the hour or the day, while others have set fees in keeping with their specialty and in line with what others in their field are charging. One of the most strenuous yet rewarding ways to work part-time is to start a business that uses your skills in a new way.

Job Security, Wherefore Art Thou?

Jobs with fizz when the economy goes flat include service-providing industry jobs involving necessity goods (e.g., food) or services (e.g., health care), luxury goods (e.g., fine jewelry for the affluent unaffected by job loss), or any of a number of other optional services.

Outmoded ideas need to be reexamined and, in all probability, even discarded. I cannot emphasize strongly enough the need to remain open-minded. I hurt and delayed myself in my job search simply because I was not fully aware of the changing scene. Understanding what is taking place will increase your likelihood of becoming reemployed and will cut down the time involved.

Other winners in a downturn in the economy are those who work in home- and auto-repair companies. Also on the most-wanted list: dental assistants, legal secretaries, and paralegals. I investigated the paralegal field and attended an information session at our local university. I was shocked to see the huge room packed with others like myself. In fact, dozens were left standing. Speakers included lawyers and paralegals themselves, and I learned that paralegals are being hired in all professions. A publisher friend wrote telling me that his wife works as a paralegal doing medical malpractice and loves it.

My point is that you must leave no stone unturned in your investigation of possibilities for yourself. Research costs you nothing except your time and energy. You may even decide to get some training in another field. Selecting a field where the opportunities might be bountiful in the years ahead is as easy as looking at areas where technological advances are being made (e.g., the environment, communications, biology, and computer technology). When you go to the U.S. Department of Labor Bureau of Labor Statistics website, you will find links to everything imaginable that will bring you up to speed very quickly. There is a lot to be learned, and this is one of the best uses of the Internet for someone deciding on a career path. (Use your Internet time wisely, or you may find that you have wasted an incredible amount of time.)

Perhaps you feel that you can't afford to go back to school or that you are too old. You are *never* too old. A friend who is taking nurse's training told me that most of the students in her class are in their midforties or older, including two women in their sixties. An evening news report showed an eighty-year-old beautician, retired for twenty years, who had just completed new training. "I'm tired of sitting around," she said. "Besides, I can't make it anymore. Folks like me, we're just living too long," she said with a big grin.

Financial assistance is offered by most universities, colleges, and trade schools, especially for those who have lost their jobs and are bumping into obstacles in their search in a particular field. Mature workers who find themselves suddenly unemployed are being offered help and retraining where necessary through a number of programs. Consult with the American Association of Retired People (AARP). Look in your Yellow Pages for a local number or use the Internet to get more information. If you don't subscribe to AARP's monthly news, consider doing so.

Recession losers tend to be workers in those industries concerned with new housing, factory machines, new cars, expensive appliances, furniture, carpeting, and other bank-loan products. At this writing, however, interest rates have been lower, and home refinancing and the purchasing of new cars and other big-ticket items have picked up considerably. I read the material that arrives each morning in *Investor's Business Daily*, which presently portrays consumer confidence remaining solid. Although this same issue says jobs are still a big concern, job prognosticators predict that new economic policies will turn around the weak job market.

At the same time, I turn to the *Dallas Morning News* weekend edition and read the headline in the Business section "Consumers Sing No-Jobs Blues." The article reports that consumer confidence is slipping because unemployment claims remain high. The scenario is being called a tug-of-war between a rising stock market and the deterioration of the job market according to a senior analyst at Lehman Brothers in New York. They ask the question, "Huh? Why aren't people feeling better about the economy?" and respond by saying, "One word: jobs!" This Dallas paper pointed out that as a result of the lack of job opportunities, 43 percent of benefits recipients are currently exhausting their benefits without finding new work, and it is the highest share on record.[4]

So I set out in my car to survey the scene throughout the greater Dallas area, and what I find doesn't surprise me. Real estate has always been a good barometer of what is happening, and on street after street, in community after community, from the Frisco/Plano area to Lewisville/Flower Mound to Grapevine/Southlake/Colleyville, For Sale signs sprout like dandelions in well-manicured yards.

"Not only is layoff activity continuing at an unrelenting pace, but people are finding it difficult to find new work," an Internet report posted on Economy.com, an economic research firm in West Chester, Pennsylvania, stated.

The much-respected columnist Joyce Lain Kennedy reminds readers that the old conventional wisdom when times are tight favors necessity industries and warns against getting into industries that make expensive things people can delay buying. The new conventional wisdom, however, says hang on to that basic common sense but add to it a recognition of unsentimental managerial attitude.

Just remember that while some markets and industries are on the downswing, others, such as health services, child care, environment, and high-tech skills, such as engineering, biochemistry, and computer expertise, are hot job markets. I urge that you follow the *Occupational Outlook Handbook*, which can be pulled up on the Internet at www.bls.gov.

The New Management View

Forget about long-term job security. Many companies today have a lean-and-mean staffing policy and will terminate your job if and when they feel you are no longer needed.

A survey of 216 major U.S. manufacturing and service firms reveals that many key entities in corporate America are moving away from business paternalism and are placing a greater emphasis on employee self-sufficiency. Under the old system, an employer would undertake to supply the needs and regulate the conduct of its employees in matters affecting them as individuals as well as in their relations to authority and to each other. This has fallen by the wayside. No longer do companies feel an obligation to look after their employees from the cradle to the grave.

That is tough to swallow, but swallow it we must. The Conference Board, a worldwide business network that conducted a study for columnist Joyce Lain Kennedy, shows that firms today are preparing for a new breed of workers who will have far less job security than in the past and who must plan their careers accordingly. The bottom line is simply this: employers want employees to understand that better compensation and continued employment are dependent on increased productivity, competitiveness, and profitability. When a company doesn't experience such gains, workers will feel it.

According to new management views, as put forward in numerous news reports and studies nationwide, companies now use what they call "targeted turnover" procedures and "phased retirement incentives," which in plain language simply means cleaning out the dead wood and encouraging employees to cut down on their hours prior to actual retirement. Never mind that you are the dead wood. It's a whole new ball game in the work world, and companies don't even seem sorry to see you move on.

Winners and Losers in Today's Job Market

If you are contemplating getting some retraining, you will benefit from following the ads in your area to get a picture of what the needs are where you live. Mobile phone companies, specialized retailers, and restaurant chains continue to hire. Minimum wages are disheartening, but if that is all you can find, then do what you have to do. Meanwhile, continue your search for better options.

Kennedy tells of a former software company CEO who had been earning $175,000 a year and then had to take a job as a mailroom clerk at $9 an hour. "Whoa—gives you the shivers!" exclaimed Kennedy.

Someone else in the same column had written her to ask what he should do to get a job in these times. He explained that his professional connections couldn't help because they were out of work too or there was a hiring freeze on at their companies. This man had withdrawn from his 401(k) account, cashed in his savings, lost his shirt on the few stocks he held, used up his unemployment, and now was walking through his house to see what he could sell on eBay. Yes, I agree with Kennedy, it does give you the shivers![5]

Still, marketing professionals who have been successful in building businesses and can prove it are in "extraordinary high demand," according to one Dallas recruiter. And all recruiting firms stress that candidates willing to relocate who can bring a fresh perspective and a proven track record have an edge. Of course, one doesn't like uprooting one's family, but if push comes to shove . . .

Tom Sawyer, whose firm Careers That Work was so helpful to me, wrote in a letter, "This country is going through some *very deep and radical* changes in the workplace. Whole industries and professions are just disappearing from the American scene." Many have already relocated in Mexico, China, and elsewhere overseas as previously pointed out.

Jack Nehlig, president of Phoenix Contact, says the biggest challenge facing manufacturers today is the trend to send manufacturing overseas. "It means less work for U.S. firms. But it can spawn innovation here, too, as displaced employees start their own businesses."[6]

But what if you can't scrape together the money to start your own business? Unemployed manufacturing engineers and design engineers are among those bearing the brunt of the flow of jobs going overseas. What is troubling is that products from integrated circuits to automobiles to medical equipment all play a role in our standard of living—many of these products are critical to our economy—and if we don't maintain some control over the design and manufacture of such products, the potential outcome is not pleasant to contemplate. The CEOs of these large companies are totally bottom-line oriented, and many continue to fatten their own portfolios at the expense of jobs for skilled workers in this country.

Electronic Engineering Times reported in a very eye-opening article entitled "Outsource Tide Won't Ebb":

> It happened in steel, in textiles, in automobiles, in electronic assembly—and now, incontrovertibly and probably irreversibly, it's happening in chip design.
>
> Chip design outsourcing is not a mere trend—a stopgap to keep companies afloat in the downturn—but a new order, a panel session at the Custom Integrated Circuits Conference concluded. . . . What's left to do, then, is sort out the

implications for the domestic industry, its engineers and, by extension, the country. Amid the free market platitudes and economic generalizations, panelists offered some guidance that may help designers find a foothold on what promises to be a slippery slope for the profession in the coming years.[7]

This redistribution of an industry that has become so much a part of the economy in this country represents a new global division of labor. It is a frightening scene for those affected, and more than one honest CEO admits that it is bad for the country. Still other CEOs argue otherwise. But the facts are indisputable. Brian Fitzgerald, chief executive of a small design services house ChipWrights, Inc., in Boston, took a macro view, but a pessimistic one, when he said that he is continually approached by overseas design shops offering to work "three to five times cheaper than we can do it here." The rising incidence of outsourcing lowers engineering salaries and career opportunities here in the United States.[8]

Fitzgerald told of engineers who need a raise, yet while he knows the men are good, they are already being paid well, and he knows he can get five times more work done for the same money offshore. "So what am I going to do?" he asks. He answers his own question: "The more we cut away at the incentives for people in the U.S. to take up engineering careers, the more we undermine our ability to innovate."[9]

These are serious concerns, and as the article stated, they cut across industries with Taiwan and China and elsewhere, collectively becoming hotbeds of activity. And where, one is tempted to ask, did so many of the foreign companies' personnel get their education? Such is the "new world order" and "global economy."

One letter writer, in response to a series of articles in the electronic magazine doing this reporting, decried what he considered a lack of concern in the White House and Congress.

I for the life of me do not understand how the loss of key technologies to offshore and potential economic and military adversaries is not raising alarms. . . . I do not understand why we, as a country, prefer to educate foreign-born students rather than our own and allow them to migrate the technologies they have learned at U.S. taxpayers' expense to their home country. . . . We could wake up one day and discover we are a Third World country.[10]

He signed his letter as a still employed engineer, but one wonders for how long! One can definitely hear alarms going off nationwide.

And what if you aren't skilled in what is so highly valued in today's workplace? And what if you aren't able to get retrained—you need a paycheck coming in as soon as possible, and you don't have energy left at day's end to go to night school? Moreover, what if jobs in what you want to do, are trained to do, and feel you do best are unavailable where you live? Or what happens if those jobs have been done away with, phased out in today's high-tech society? These questions will be addressed in an endeavor to shed light on the options available.

"Truly Revolutionary"

In *Powershift* Alvin Toffler makes the point that changes have come and will continue to come as a result of the clashes of a "most unholy trinity: knowledge, wealth, and violence." He predicts that power will shift increasingly to those best at "information judo"—people who can capitalize on technology, new discoveries, databases, competitors' secrets, and other kinds of knowledge.

But, says Toffler, because information "can be grasped by the weak and the poor as well as the strong and the rich, the change is truly revolutionary." Information is permanently subversive, "a continuing threat to the powerful."[11] If you can turn knowledge to your advantage, you will discover in this revolutionary time that the rich and strong don't always win in this kind of game.

And talk about violence! The world is not the same as it was before 9/11. Life can be scary, but before you panic, don't forget who is in control. As J. B. Phillips was so fond of saying, God is not an absentee omnipotent. One of the great qualities that New Testament Christianity exhibits is hope (see, e.g., Rom. 15:13). "In the New Testament writings there is a continual sense not only of the immediacy but of the contemporaneousness of God." The tendency of many today is to put God in the past. How ridiculous! "Our urgent need is to discover God, the God of hope, in the present strain, in the complex problem, actually at work in the given situation. For He is either a present help or He is not much help at all."[12] We need to keep our focus on the God of hope.

Let's face it—we can no longer simply blame a recession for job loss. Recessions come and recessions go. Something more is taking place. While a recession may account for some unemployment figures, it is but a blip on the screen of what is actually a long-term trend in corporate organizations, brought on, for one thing, by heightened competition in the global marketplace, instantaneous communication, and ecological limits. The result of all this is a mighty extrusion of personnel. That means exit you, your neighbor, possibly one or more of your children, your friends, and me. It is a squeeze-out that calls for wise decision making on your part as you contemplate what to do next.

Is It Possible to Become a Mover and a Shaker in the Future?

Movers and shakers of the future, regardless of their age, will be those who understand the competitive world we are now living in and are willing to confront it. The world today is far different than it was even ten years ago. It is now an international world. As one executive said, "It's going to be Singapore to Sydney and Paris, not Los Angeles, Denver, and Chicago."

Analysts agree. An appreciation of world cultures will help speed the climb on corporate ladders. One thing that will enable some individuals to get an edge is to have studied another language. That itself may open up some ideas for you as you contemplate future alternatives, so give it serious thought.

Go to the library and examine classified ads from newspapers in other parts of the country. Don't underestimate the value of using the library in your search for information on what is happening nationwide. I have had many people thank me for urging them to do this. "My eyes were really opened," they have said. Job prospects in your particular field may be very promising elsewhere. If you aren't willing to move and make some big changes, you may have to ride out hard times and opt for something else. Avoid procrastination. Fear keeps many job seekers from getting started, but making excuses will only prolong your agony. Hopefully, this book will help you overcome your inertia if in fact procrastination is a problem.

Learn to Play by the New Rules

New rules are governing the corporate workplace. For example, some companies have adopted the 1/2 by 2 by 3 rule of corporate fitness: half as many people on the payroll being paid twice as well, producing three times as much. This, along with the many other factors discussed in this chapter, is contributing to the reconfiguration of the workplace, requiring that we rethink our old assumptions. We must begin to think differently about who we are, what we do, and where we are going to do it.

Let's accept the challenge and do all within our control to bring order and stability to our lives. Then we must trust God to do for us what we can't do for ourselves.

God didn't get knocked off his throne; you just got knocked off your job. The executioner's song is never a lullaby. So when the grim reaper wielding the ax announces, "Wham bang, you're out the door," what can you do? How can you respond so as to minimize the bad effects and maximize what you have going for you? Answers to these questions can be found in the next chapter.

2

The First Things to Do
(or Consider Doing)

Stephen Covey, in *The Seven Habits of Highly Effective People*, paraphrases Management guru Peter Drucker: "Effective people are not problem-minded; they're opportunity-minded. They feed opportunities and starve problems."[1] Covey goes on to cite E. M. Gray's essay "The Common Denominator of Success," which I read and benefited from soon after losing my job. "The successful person has the habit of doing the things failures don't like to do. They don't like doing them either necessarily. But their disliking is subordinated to the strength of their purpose."[2]

Gray's words reinforced a principle I had put into place in my life many years before: if anything of value was to be accomplished in my life, it wasn't going to be handed to me on a silver platter. It would come by dint of self-discipline, subordinating desires, feelings, impulses, and moods to inner values. Whatever it was that needed doing, I had to get to work and do it—whether I felt like it or not—and be willing to consider employment in a job that wasn't necessarily my preference.

Focusing on What Matters Most Right Now

Perhaps panic has caused you to be frozen into inaction or, even worse, to take inappropriate action. Your nerve and creativity are immobilized by your sudden derailment. You need a game plan, but you don't have the emotional energy to get one going. Your mind is in overload.

I know those feelings! And I have put together a checklist to help you move from inaction to positive action. Below are sixteen things to do or consider doing after losing your job. If some don't apply to you, skip them. Concentrate on those that do apply. If you have already done some of these things, great! Move on to the rest of the list. Perhaps you will find a few things you haven't done or thought of doing. Think of this as feeding opportunities and starving problems and doubts.

1. *Contact the Department of Employment and Training Services.* Get out your phone book and look up the address if you don't already know it. Every locality will have its own way of listing government services. Look under that terminology (e.g., GOVERNMENT) in your phone book; it is usually found before the Yellow Pages section. Then carefully scrutinize the information provided. You may end up calling more than one department. Don't get discouraged; keep at it until you find someone who can help you. Before driving over, phone and ask questions:

- Do I qualify for unemployment insurance? (They will ask you some questions to make that determination.)
- When is the earliest I can apply?
- What is the waiting period?

Appendix A has additional information on unemployment insurance.

2. *Be conservative.* Set in motion in your thinking, as well as in the thinking of family members, the idea of being conservative. That is why I suggested you phone the Department of Employment before driving there. I waited more than an hour standing in line at the Department of Employment only to find out information I could have learned with one phone call. I left very frustrated, my nerves on edge.

Let your fingers do the walking whenever possible. Combine trips to the store, the post office, wherever. Conserve your time, gas, mileage, and wear and tear on your car. Most of all, conserve your nerves.

3. *Have a family conference.* If you are the breadwinner—male or female—you need to call a family conference. I know you don't want to burden your children, but family members need to know what is happening. Show your children how their responses and actions can help ease everyone through this transition time.

Carefully think through what you will say. This is an opportunity for you to demonstrate faith, strength, and reliance on God, and that same opportunity belongs to your family. You are in this together.

Our children are grown, and most of them have families of their own. At the time of my job loss, my husband and I were living in the Midwest and all of our family lived on the West Coast. But we informed our sons, daughters, and grandchildren by phone calls or letters, and we kept them apprised of our situation on a regular basis. Why? We valued their concern, their expressions of love, and especially their prayers.

Even more important, we knew that at some point our prayers would be answered, and we wanted our children and especially our grandchildren to see that God does answer their prayers. Don't deprive your children and, if you have them, your grandchildren of this. Here is an opportunity for spiritual growth for them as well as for you.

4. *Make provisions for health insurance.* You may have been given an extension of health insurance benefits with your severance package, but at some point they will expire. Be aware of the government-mandated COBRA plan, which permits workers to buy coverage under a former employer's health plan for an average of eighteen months after leaving the company. Appendix A has additional information.

5. *Talk with your former employer.* Consider whether there would be some advantage to going back to your former employer and asking, in light of your good work performance, if any part-time work is available. Perhaps they could use your services as a consultant.

6. *Consider the circumstances that led to your unemployment.* You may need to investigate your legal rights and consult with a lawyer. The Department of Employment can advise you. I chose not to see a lawyer even though I had dozens of people advising me that I should (including people at the Department of Employment). For some, a conflict arises because of biblical beliefs (see 1 Cor. 6:1–8). In retrospect, to spare others the pain of the prolonged job loss I experienced, I should have cooperated with the local Department of Employment, whose intentions were to stop an unethical practice at the organization where I had worked.

7. *Make sure your former employer was fair in financial compensation.* Did you receive everything that was due you when you lost your job? What about unpaid vacation time? How about employee stock ownership benefits? Was money accruing in a life insurance plan? (You may want to borrow on life insurance; some people told me this is what they did.)

8. *Think entrepreneurially.* Consider marketing your services with a business card and/or other printed information. Many people do this successfully.

9. *Make an appointment with your banker.* Explain what has happened and assure him or her that you want to maintain your integrity. An astute banker will appreciate your honesty. Ours did. She worked with us every step of the way.

10. *Notify your creditors.* If it appears that you will fall behind or not be able to pay your bills, be up-front and honest. You will accomplish far more by doing this than by skipping payments and getting behind and putting your credit standing in jeopardy.

11. *Reserve your available bank card credit as a last resort.* If using credit becomes a necessity, be very careful and judicious.

12. *Consider tapping into home equity.* Some people use this as a means of keeping the roof over their heads and bread on the table. Talk it over with your mortgage company, but do everything possible to hang on to your home if it represents a substantial investment.

13. *Organize your finances.* Cut back and cut out. Eliminate unnecessary expenditures. Practice frugality. Do without. See chapter 5 for additional things you can do to make the best of your financial status.

14. *Consider part-time, evening, or temporary work.* Temping is fast becoming one of the best ways to earn a living. Often, working as a temporary can lead to a good full-time position. Don't dismiss this as a viable way to go.

Temping has become a permanent feature of our postindustrial society. For an indication of the increasing importance of temporary employment services, turn to the Yellow Pages of your local telephone directory. Temporary services aren't just for office workers anymore. They are for accountants, comparison shoppers, doctors, draftsmen, engineers, factory assemblers, health care technicians, lawyers, survey takers, telephone orderers, warehouse workers, people who hand out samples in supermarkets, to name a few.

Today's temporary services have training programs designed to enhance the skill levels of their help for hire. I have talked to dozens of people who have sought temporary positions precisely because these agencies have provided them with hands-on training in computer operation, including word processing and other software. In today's market climate, one has to be computer literate.

Moreover, some temporary services now offer benefit packages for employees who work a specific number of hours. The steady pay, flexibility, and benefits of temping could be a winning combination to see you through your job-loss crisis.

Once thought of as companies to call when a secretary had the flu or a bookkeeper was on vacation, temporary agencies have changed dramatically. Experienced and skilled professionals from a variety of professions are turning to temp agencies. Remember, this is one of the largest growth industries throughout the country.

According to Stacey Burke, spokesperson for Labor Ready, "manufacturing hiring is one of the first areas of the labor market to shine,"[3] when there is improvement, for instance, in the manufacturing sector.

Others say, however, that the increased use of temporary workers is a sign that firms are starting to treat labor as a variable rather than a fixed cost, which means that rising temporary employment may no longer be a clear sign of full-time hiring. "There is a fundamental change taking place in the labor market," says David Rosenberg, chief North America economist at Merrill Lynch. "The price of labor is being forced to adjust to the cost of capital. The U.S. labor market is not only repricing itself to India and China, but also to the declining cost of capital in the U.S."

He points to employment costs that have risen 75 percent since 1988. "What's risen most are these runaway benefit costs—medical care, pension fund contributions and workmen's comp."

Once again the facts present themselves: companies have found that hiring temporary workers saves them money and lets them be more flexible. "It's a cost-saving method for business to ride out a period of stronger-than-expected demand without having to bloat their labor cost bills. It's all telling the same story of change in corporate management labor practices to save costs and boost margins. That's what the game is all about," Rosenberg says.[4]

15. *Look for work in nonobvious places.* Investigate companies smaller than the one where you were employed. As corporate America slashes away at its payrolls, more professionals are putting their careers in perspective by thinking small. You might consider working for a smaller company a demotion, but you could be very pleasantly surprised. You may even find it an exhilarating experience. In general, small businesses have weathered the economic storms far better than corporate counterparts, providing superior job prospects in such industries as printing and publishing, health care services, computer and data processing, and many others.

16. *Be flexible and willing to relocate.* Your family may object to a move, but you will have to be firm and educate them about the realities of life. One study by an outplacement firm shows that job seekers who were willing to relocate saw an increase in compensation. This same report shows that some of the best employment opportunities are with companies that are themselves in the process of relocating.

You will find some of these points discussed in greater detail in subsequent chapters. What is important now is that you get started, and this checklist is a good place to begin. The sooner you take positive steps, the sooner you will start to see progress in your situation.

3

Private Victories
Precede Public Victories

As first Lord of the Admiralty, Winston Churchill was personally blamed for the costly Dardanelles disaster and forced to resign. Even after successfully steering his country through yet another war, his countrymen rejected him at the polls. Yet he remained undaunted and rose again to be the Prime Minister of England in her darkest hour. He died the most esteemed man in his generation.[1]

Imagine it: Churchill forced to resign. Some of you probably found yourselves in the same kind of situation. What was Churchill's reaction? Did he allow his adversities to dominate his thoughts and keep him from moving on? No, history faithfully records that he remained undaunted.

Covey suggests that rather than focusing on the weaknesses of other people and the circumstances that were responsible for our present situation, we instead should start with a new level of thinking. Valuable time, effort, and energy can be lost when your focus is askew. Constantly looking back at what has happened and wondering *What if?* will, in the long run, short-circuit what will work for your benefit from this point on. You will waste a lot of emotional energy in the days ahead if your thinking is inappropriately focused. How can you move your thinking process along so you can make progress in a new direction?

Covey recommends an "inside-out" approach to acquire a new level of thinking. In all his experience, he says, he has never seen lasting solutions to problems, lasting happiness and success, that came from the outside in.[2] This is in keeping with what the apostle Paul said when he wrote that we are to be transformed by the renewing of our minds (see Rom. 12:2). Appropriate responses to any situation result when we allow this to happen.

If the inner life is to be nurtured and the outer life is to give evidence of being under the control of the Holy Spirit, then we must seek to be continually spiritually receptive. We need a divine infusion of wisdom and discernment as we go through this crisis.

Don't worry about anything; instead pray about everything; tell God your needs and don't forget to thank him for his answers. If you do this you will experience God's peace, which is far more wonderful than the human mind can understand. His peace will keep your thoughts and your hearts quiet and at rest as you trust in Christ Jesus. . . . Fix your thoughts on what is true and good and right. Think about things that are pure and lovely, and dwell on the fine, good things in others. Think about all you can praise God for and be glad about.

Philippians 4:6–8 TLB

Inventory the Good Things

A good exercise to help you think about all you can praise God for and be glad about is to write down the good and right things you have going in your life. Hopefully, you now have a better grasp on what may have contributed to your job loss, so it's time for some attitude refocusing. Why not begin by thanking God for the good things and asking him for his help in turning your present situation into something good?

After my own job loss, I was able to shift my mind into the mode of taking stock. I had a wonderfully supportive husband, great children, and adoring grandchildren. I still had friends. I had a little sense of humor left. Moreover, I had my health. Although I had queasiness in the pit of my stomach (nerves reacting) and a light-headed feeling, I hadn't had a heart attack, I didn't have some awful disease, and I could respond favorably when my husband said, "Let's get something to eat."

We had many other things going for us that I was able to enumerate in the days ahead, and you will be able to do so also. Why don't you take a few moments right now and begin your own list of good things? Think in terms of values, skills, and gifts. If you need help, ask a loved one who can mirror back for you what he or she sees.

Your present unemployment is but a part of the landscape called your life. You won't be where you are now forever. The painting isn't finished yet. The Master Artist has the total picture in mind. He knows the end from the beginning, and you are important to him. This is but a part of a great whole. Who knows what good can come out of all this? God does! Dare to believe that the rest is going to be far better than what is past.

Allow Yourself Time

Remind yourself often to give yourself time. Give God time. Recognize that it may take a while to untangle the tangles that have appeared in the skein of your life. Be patient toward all that is unsolved. Diamonds don't form overnight. We all are in process; we are not finished products yet. Searching for three to five months *or more* for the right job is not unusual. My own job search took seventeen months, and I sent out more than a thousand resumes. For those searching for an executive position, the search may indeed be extensive. One prominent northern California physicist told me that he sent out more than two thousand resumes with well-crafted cover letters and waited two years to be hired. Someone else told me that a CEO friend sent out more than three thousand resumes.

This is not meant to discourage you. The point is, you must be realistic, get your expectations in line, make wise decisions, set goals, organize your finances, publicize your job search through networking and in other appropriate ways, avoid making snap decisions, and seek ways to turn this time into a positive contribution for the future. Turning a bad situation into a good one takes research and preparation. Your first priority should be to establish in your mind that looking for a new job is going to be your present job.

Prepare Yourself for the Search

I found job hunting to be exhausting, and it took a lot of courage. Some days I felt totally zapped. If it had not been for Scriptures that I recalled, my confidence would have been so sapped, my energy so depleted, I doubt I could have pressed on.

The temptation to wallow in self-pity and succumb to ongoing anger plagued me for a long time. I had to put forth tremendous effort to keep from caving in. Each day I got up, dressed comfortably, applied my makeup, and looked professional. One man told me he got up, showered, shaved, and put on his business suit and tie: "Then I raced for the front door, grabbed the paper off the step, headed for the coffeepot, sat down, opened the paper to the classifieds and the business section and got to work."

You are going to feel like a failure. I did. But failure, if you want to call job loss that, is not final. I learned a lot from this experience, and so will you if you will embrace the pain, invite it in, and make peace with it. When we do that, the painful experience is no longer pointless. I determined that with God's help I would not waste my unemployment. I would learn everything I could from it. Moreover, I would pass on what I learned to others. And that is how this book came about.

When we see successful people, we may assume that they got all the breaks, that they were always in the right place at the right time, that they have never failed, that they have never been rejected. The truth is, few people accomplish what they hope to achieve the first time they attempt it. Even the most successful people generally have a checkerboard career of both success and failure.

Look at Winston Churchill, mentioned at the outset of this chapter, and at the poet Robert Frost, who was considered a failure for more than twenty years. Today Frost towers as one of America's greatest verse writers, a four-time winner of the coveted Pulitzer prize, with poems published in twenty-two languages. Or one could look at Alexander Graham Bell, who suffered one humiliating setback after another. He spent much of his life being laughed at and ridiculed. Nobody laughs at Bell today! In the early years, Walt Disney went around Hollywood with his cartoon ideas a bankrupt man. By all normal standards, he was a failure. And how many know that Johnny Carson's first effort at his own network show was a miserable flop?

Arthur Gordon, author of *A Touch of Wonder*, tells about Thomas J. Watson, president of International Business Machines, who gave some invaluable advice to a struggling writer who had received many rejections:

You're making a common mistake. You're thinking of failure as the enemy of success. But it isn't that at all. Failure is a teacher—a harsh one, perhaps, but the best. . . . You've got to put failure to work for you. You can be discouraged by failure—or you can learn from it. So go ahead and make mistakes. Make all you can. Because, remember, that's where you'll find success. On the far side of failure.[3]

Start with Private Victories

As part of his doctoral program, Stephen Covey began a search in the 1970s of all the success literature. The inspiration and wisdom of many thinkers resulted, among other things, in the development of his book *The Seven Habits of Highly Effective People*. Out of all this research, one of Covey's many discoveries was that private victories always precede public victories. He speaks of the power of a "paradigm shift"—what one might call the "Aha!" experience when someone finally sees the composite picture in another way. The more bound a person is by the initial perception, the more powerful the "Aha!" experience is. "It's as though a light were suddenly turned on in the inside," Covey says.

The word *paradigm* comes from the Greek. The way it is used here refers to the way we see the world—not in terms of our visual sight, but in terms of perceiving, understanding, interpreting. A simple way to understand paradigms is to see them as maps. "Each of us has many, many maps in our head," explains Covey, "which can be divided into two main categories: maps of *the ways things are*, or *realities*, and maps of *the way things should be*, or *values*. We interpret everything we experience through these mental maps. We seldom question their accuracy; we're usually even unaware that we have them. We simply *assume* that the way we see things is the way they really are or the way they should be."[4]

Attitudes and behaviors grow out of those assumptions, whether correct or incorrect. The way we see things affects the way we think and the way we act. This has a direct bearing on our relationships. When we are faced with sudden unemployment and all its ramifications, we need a dramatic paradigm shift, and it must come from the inside out.

David Knuth, an unemployed engineer, writing in *Electronic Engineering Times*, talked about fending off despair as being half the battle as it chipped away at his self-esteem. He slumped into self-pity for a few days, and his focus became clouded. "Sitting in the same room as my family, I would be miles away inside my head. But support from others would help me pull my focus off myself. As if a fever broke, hope would return and I would become myself again."

He spoke of encouragement coming through both helpful intentions and tangible means from other people. With friends, neighbors, former colleagues, his church family, and extended family assisting in a variety of ways, including prayer and offers of financial assistance, his attitude began to shift. Through a remarkable series of events, he won a trip to a conference in San Francisco where he reconnected with other engineers. "Though I didn't come home with a job, I came back as a confident embedded-systems engineer who just happens to be looking for work. Those rogue thoughts of before are nowhere to be found . . ."

He concluded, "I continue to look forward to what's next on this journey, whether it is growing my company or becoming an employee of another one. The journey—not the destination—is what matters, because this is where life is lived. A passage from the Bible best describes this episode of my journey: '. . . tribulation produces perseverance; and perseverance, character; and character, hope. Now hope does not disappoint.'"[5] Knuth experienced a major paradigm shift. How illustrative this is of what hope can do for a person.

You and I know the wisdom that comes from the Bible will always be superior to any human thinking. There we are told that as a man thinks in his heart, so he is (Prov. 23:7). We are reminded to keep our hearts with all diligence, for out of it flow the issues of life (Prov. 4:23). In these and hundreds of similar admonitions, we discover that God will prepare our minds for action, giving us self-control and the wisdom and discernment to know how to respond to the crises that job loss imposes. Moreover, when we seek God's help, patiently trusting him, we can be hopeful. Yes, private victories do precede public victories.

With the apostle Paul, let us say, "I am ready for anything through the strength of the one who lives within me" (Phil. 4:13 Phillips).

4

Be a Master, Not a Victim, of Your Situation

When it happens to you, all you hear is that you've been canned, dismissed, terminated, pink-slipped, or fired. Society has all kinds of nice-sounding euphemisms to describe the loss of one's job.

*U*nemployed! The word echoes in your head: *Unemployed! Unemployed!*

Perhaps you were told the company was "downsizing." Sounds nice. Better than "You're fired!" You may have fallen victim to a merger, a takeover, or restructuring. Maybe the place where you were employed went out of business. Perhaps massive layoffs were necessary. Age discrimination, sex discrimination, or race discrimination may have been involved.

Years ago, and it has remained a part of my thinking, someone said we live in a culture where the job defines the individual. How true that is! You meet someone new, and

51

he or she asks, "What do you do?" Think about that—when you lose a job, your identity as defined by society gets stripped from you, particularly if you've been fired. This person said, "You become vocationally naked, and that feels bad." Pretty potent words!

No matter what you call it, it's painful. Traumatic. Scary. Devastating. None of these words is an exaggeration. You could add to this, I'm sure. Be my guest. Voice to yourself how it felt to lose your vocational identity or how you may be feeling about it right now. Spit out the words. Purge your pain.

If I could hear you, nothing you'd say could shock me. I have experienced all the emotions you have felt or are feeling: *denial*, "Oh no! This can't be happening to me!"; *isolation*, "I wish I could just run away or climb under the covers and not have to face another day"; *anger*, "I am *so* angry. I've never felt such anger"; *bargaining*, "God, if you will just help me find another job, I'll _____ [fill in the blank]"; *depression*, "I can't stand another day of this uncertainty"; and *despair*, "This is so immobilizing."

The day will come, however, when all this will be behind you. You will experience acceptance in a new job and move on to better things.

Job Loss Has Many Faces

Job loss is no respecter of persons. In fact, it may wear a familiar face—the face of your husband or wife, a child, a neighbor, or a friend.

I certainly didn't expect to become unemployed after being recruited for a ministry management position and moving across the country. Let me share the story of what happened to me. The following is a late-night call I placed to a friend in Southern California on the day I lost my job.

"Hi, Barb! How are things?"

"Well, hi to you. What in the world are you doing calling me at this hour of the night? It's midnight where you are, isn't it?"

"Well, yes, but I can sleep in tomorrow morning."

"What did you say? What do you mean? Tomorrow's Thursday. You can't sleep in on a weekday."

"Well, sure. Sure I can. It's like this. I lost my job today."

Silence.

"Hello . . . hello, Barb? Are you there?"

"You lost your job? You couldn't have lost your job. The company paid thousands of dollars to move you out there not too long ago. You didn't ask for that job. You're valuable to them. You made a sacrifice to go out there. Look at all the good things you've produced. Tell me it's a joke."

"No joke, Barb. I'm well into my third year here. That is, I *was* into my third year."

"So you really lost your job today. What happened?"

"They're slashing, so they said."

"Slashing?"

"That's the word, like in cutting, and I got cut. There will be a lot more. At least that's what they said . . ."

"But what are you going to do?"

"I've started a list. I'll be adding to it as I go."

"A list?"

"Like a grocery list; only mine reads: (1) Go to the unemployment office, wherever that is. I've barely learned my way around this town, let alone where the unemployment office is. But I'll find it. (2) Update my resume. (3) Figure out where I should send my resume. (4) Write cover letters to accompany my resumes. (5) Make telephone calls. They call it networking. (6) Start watching the newspaper want ads."

"It all sounds like work to me."

"I know, but that's what I need—work, as in a good paying job. So in order to find another job, I've got to get to work here at home."

"Are you going to be up to it?"

"It's three weeks between us and whatever . . ."

"What do you mean, three weeks?"

"Severance, Barb. You haven't been gainfully employed for a long time, have you?"

"You mean you only received three weeks' severance pay?"

"Yes." [*Sigh*.] "And no vacation pay. And only three more weeks of medical coverage."

"I heard that sigh."

"Two thousand miles away and you heard me sigh over the phone?"

"I have good hearing. What aren't you telling me that I think I detected in the sigh?"

"How old are you, Barb?"

"You know better than to ask. Shirley Temple, you, and I are the same age. You know that."

"Sure do. And I'm not Shirley Temple."

"Are you scared?"

"Probably . . . Well, yes. I haven't had much time to think about it. It will probably hit me tomorrow. Still, I feel . . . How do I describe it? Calm? Peaceful?"

"You're in a state of shock, although you sound okay, except for that sigh. You weren't expecting this, were you? How do you explain how you feel?"

"No, I wasn't expecting this. It came as a total surprise. I mean, Barb, just think, I'm suddenly unemployed. Did I mention there's a seventh thing on my list?"

"Want me to guess?"

"No, I want to tell you. Number 7 is trust God and pray."

"I'll be praying for you."

"I know you will, and that's why I called. I'll need your prayers."

"You can count on them. I love you, Helen."

Reach Out for Someone's Touch

I could count on Barb and others like her from coast to coast. My husband and I experienced an incredible outpouring of love and concern.

Have you reached out for someone's touch? Right now you need affirming, kind words. Have you received them from someone?

One of the right responses to your situation is to swallow your pride and allow others the privilege of showing you how much they care. Sharing in others' pain is a privilege, although some may not recognize this. The fact is, someone else's job loss collides with our conscience. Yet to stand alongside someone who is experiencing job loss trauma is every bit as important as standing by someone who has experienced loss through death or divorce.

We often see writers pointing out how society and our government blame the victims of unemployment for their plight. An outpouring of sympathy and support takes place when a person becomes critically ill or loses his home through fire or a tornado, but the reaction is very often quite different when a person's livelihood is taken away through unemployment. Of course, some people are unemployed primarily because they are lazy or irresponsible, but these people make up a small minority. The truth is, millions of hardworking people lose their jobs through no fault of their own.

Because our situation is so frequently misunderstood, sometimes spiritual platitudes are spouted at us by well-meaning, but almost totally uninformed, individuals. It is good to be reminded that God is faithful, but "nice little plastic spiritual phrases don't help people unlock their grief," my friend Barbara Johnson says. "It is better to just put your arm around a grieving person [and yes, job loss involves a grieving process] and say, 'I love you—God loves you.' Beyond that, it might be best to just shove a sock in your mouth and keep quiet. . . . The simple truth is this: *When grief is the freshest, words should be the fewest.*"

People I talked to told me that after prolonged unemployment they would equate job loss with death. "In death there is closure," said one friend who had experienced both job loss and death in the family. "In sustained job loss the problems become enormously complex."

Typical Problems Encountered and Questions Asked

We run into a variety of problems when our unemployment goes beyond what is considered the norm (that "norm" varies according to various reports). If we know what to expect, we can let those around us know how they can help. At the time of my job loss, I corresponded with writer Richard Bolles, who said to expect the job hunt to be quite long. He pointed to experienced outplacement people who claimed the job hunt could take one month for every $10,000 of salary someone is seeking. At the time I lost my job, the job hunt in the United States typically lasted somewhere between eight and twenty-three weeks. Much depends on the state of the economy, the age of the job hunter, and how that person is aiming. In any event, Bolles cautioned me not to count on the eight-week minimum but to be mentally prepared for the twenty-three.

Columnist Joyce Lain Kennedy calls that $10,000 salary bit "an old chestnut that's been around a long time," adding that its credibility is elusive. Bolles maintained that this statistic could only survive because it fits what people know from their own experience or the experience of others. In other words, it hasn't been disproved. The real answer is that the timing depends on how hard and how smart you work at the job search. A key is to work smarter not harder!

The importance of friends and family who understand cannot be stressed enough. You're fortunate if you are married to someone who can help you put things in perspective. Not everyone has that advantage. Job loss can be very hard on a marriage. If you are married and are encountering problems with your relationship as a result of unemployment, consider seeking some counseling.

Of all the gifts that God gives to sustain and nourish our lives, none can equal the presence of a faithful friend. What would we do without friends? Professionals in the field of counseling say that there is perhaps no more effective way to relieve psychic pain than to be in contact with other human beings who understand what you are going through. That can be relatives, friends, neighbors, a pastor or priest, or a professional counselor. Have you confided in someone you can trust? Someone you know who loves and understands you?

I could be candid with most of our friends, knowing my words were not falling on deaf or insensitive ears. Be honest with your friends and whomever you choose as a confidant. Let your hair down. You don't have to be ashamed if you have lost your job. Apologies and explanations that border on being overly defensive aren't necessary. Just be yourself.

Often the "But why?" question will erupt from the lips of family and friends who may call into question why you are without a job. People like this don't seem particularly sensitive and empathetic to what has happened to you. I know that can hurt. One friend, impatient with my inability to find the right position, and not fully understanding all the reasons for this, blurted out one day, "Well, why do you have to go for such a high-powered job? That's your mistake. Settle for something else." In truth, I wasn't doing that. My kind of work may be considered "high-powered" or "high-visibility," but I wasn't seeking something beyond my capabilities. Her hurtful remark was a clear example of the misconceptions people may have. Never mind. Move on.

You don't need someone critically assessing you right now. I didn't need it either. What can you do? I'm big on subtracting from my problems wherever I can. You can do that too. When we had encounters with negative friends or persons with somewhat abrasive personalities, I made it a point to be positive. I sought God's help, asking him to infuse me with a growing faith that would reflect my confidence that he was in this with me.

I'm happy to be able to tell you that my attitude got noticed. More than one person who had conveyed a questioning attitude toward me changed—sometimes in subtle, but nevertheless, unmistakable ways. I heard several times, "You seem so hopeful. What's happening?"

"I'm trusting God," I'd say, "and doing what I believe are the right things to bring about some good results."

But I didn't lie. I'm made of dust, and some days I'm dustier than others. When I was downhearted, I admitted it. I'd answer questions with words to this effect: "Frankly, it's tough at times. Things aren't easy right now. Not much has happened. In fact, I don't have anything to report except that I'm treating this interim as a full-time job."

In the process of seeking reemployment, we made a move back to the West Coast, where my husband, who was semi-retired, had been offered a part-time position as an associate pastor. One weekend when I was out of the city on a writing assignment, a woman asked my husband where I was. When told, she commented, "There are some of us who feel your wife should be assisting you—making hospital and home visitation calls and doing more."

My husband and I both understood that job hunting is *not* something to just do on the side. Some people may think your present situation indicates that you have time on your hands. They may try to impinge on it. Don't hold the erroneous attitudes of friends and family against them. Not everyone can identify with what it means to be unemployed.

One of the saddest stories that came to my attention concerned a husband and wife team who both lost their jobs. They couldn't bring themselves to share their misfortune with anyone—not even family members. It was only when they were evicted from their home that family and neighbors knew there was a problem.

In contrast to this, my editor told me of one suddenly unemployed couple who immediately called their best friends. The friends said, "Hold everything. We're coming over with pizza." Tearfully the couple spilled out their pained reactions while their friends wrapped their arms around them and patted them on the back—loving gestures that conveyed, "We're in this with you. You can count on us."

One woman told of her experience as she recalled her feelings immediately after being told, "Sorry, it's not working out," and being handed her termination papers. "Five minutes ago I thought I was a valuable executive," she said. "Now I am a defective product being recalled from the shelves. A supermarket aisle recedes into the distance. Unfit for consumption, I am briskly wheeled away to the loading dock while marketing experts decide how to present the story to the press."

Her words and reaction don't impress me as being an exaggeration. My own reaction felt like I was holding my breaking heart and my breath in check at the same time. Often a phone call or a note of encouragement from a friend helped pick me up.

So if you are a friend, family member, or neighbor of someone who is suddenly unemployed, be available. You don't have to have profound words of wisdom to offer. Your affirming presence is what is needed the most. Assure the person you care about that you are holding him or her close in thought.

Risky Business

If you're unemployed and needing support from others, the step of self-disclosure can be risky. Facing the misunderstanding of one's friends or family can be devastating. Hopefully, you know who your real friends are. Honesty literally can be a health insurance policy, because honesty promotes health and friendship. Most of us truly do like people who reveal themselves to us. So if you are willing to be open and honest, you will connect with people who cannot keep from loving you.

Take note, you who are reading this and know someone who is unemployed: the impact of prayers, cards, letters, phone calls, personal visits, gifts, invitations to eat out, and whatever else you can think of will be enormous, helping to strengthen and encourage your friends.

I'll always remember what our friends did for us on Valentine's Day, our anniversary, while we were job hunting in California. Our home had been put on the market in the Midwest, and we had left with just some clothes in our suitcases and my computer, printer, working files, and books. We received a Valentine-anniversary card signed by our friends that included little personal notes on heart-shaped pieces of paper they had gone to the trouble to cut out. Their gift to us had been to go to our home and spend the day dusting, vacuuming, and polishing, to "make it smell pretty like it always did when you were here." The house had stood vacant seven months by then and needed some TLC (tender loving care). Their thoughtful act encouraged my husband and me immensely.

You May Need to Lower Your Expectations

Note, however, that there are some things your friends cannot do for you. And don't blame them for this. Your friends should not be expected to bail you out of the financial dilemma caused by your job loss. To expect that is to expect too much.[1]

My husband and I decided at the outset that our problems were not the problems of others. Even though we shared our dilemma with others because they asked us to be very candid, we decided that we would assume responsibility for our welfare and, with God's help, find ways to meet our needs. If financial help or other assistance came, we would be extremely grateful. But we would not expect it. By lowering our expectations or, to be more accurate, by setting them in line with what we knew squared with human nature, we were spared additional heartache and disappointment.

Love: Like Putting Money in the Bank

If you are a friend or family member of an unemployed person and you have it within your means to come to the aid of someone you care about who has experienced job loss, please do what you can. And give your assistance without expectation of being paid back. Show your loved one that your relationship has no strings attached. The Bible speaks of friends as loving at all times and says that a brother is born for adversity (see Prov. 17:17).

If you're reading this because you know someone who has experienced job loss, please don't be judgmental of the person and his situation. The last thing an unemployed person needs is someone raising questions and doubts in his mind. His emotional burden is already enormous. Practice the art of affirmation. Learn how to give it and give it generously. That kind of giving doesn't require that you reach into your wallet or pull out your checkbook.

When you give through such heartwarming things as hugs and kind words, it's like putting love in the bank. You will gain interest on it for the future when you need it, and you never know when that might be. You too, heaven forbid, may experience job loss at some point in your life.

Your Greatest Source of Help

Throughout my unemployment, my husband and I discovered that there is one source of help that will never disappoint you. On the basis of much tested experience, I can assure you that in God we have a friend who the Bible tells us sticks closer than a brother (Prov. 18:24).

Your greatest source of help and hope is what he alone can supply. He is the one who affirms us beyond all others, the one who knows all the possibilities that lie deep within us. He is the one who loves us when we, in our pain, refuse to or cannot love ourselves or are immobilized by our present plight. He is the one who cherishes us. What he offers will be a kind of love-glue that will hold you together.

It is important that you not walk alone. To see most clearly where we are headed, we must walk with a sense of commitment to and trust in those with whom we are walking. In being loved by God and others, we will be affirmed and will likely be strengthened and transformed when we open ourselves to what is being offered.

Regardless of where you stand in your relationship with God, here is an opportunity for you to open yourself up to him. While looking in the Bible for ongoing help, one day I discovered something in the apostle Paul's life that spoke to my heart. Paul's life was drawing to a close, and he knew it, so he wrote a letter to young Timothy, his son in the faith. What a powerful document that letter is.

Paul was a prisoner in chains before Nero, a vile man. He wrote, "At my first defense no one stood with me, but all forsook me. May it not be charged against them" (2 Tim. 4:16). Where were the stalwart Roman saints? His dearest friends, it seemed, had deserted him. But wait! Not all. For

Paul wrote, "But the Lord stood with me and strengthened me" (v. 17). That, my friend, is the kind of support we have from God.

This is not pie-in-the-sky kind of thinking. This is present reality. God is saying to you, as he said to me, "Trust me. Walk on. I am going to lead you into something new." He *will* do for you what you cannot do for yourself. Seize this as a moment of opportunity to demonstrate a strong and steady trust. Psalm 42:11 reminds us to hope in God:

> Why are you cast down, O my soul?
> And why are you disquieted within me?
> Hope in God;
> For I shall yet praise Him,
> The help of my countenance and my God.

Oh, remember this: There is never a time when we may not hope in God. Whatever our necessities, however great our difficulties, and though to all appearances hope is impossible, yet our business is to hope in God, and it will be found that it is not in vain. In the Lord's own time help will come.

George Mueller

5

Where Do You Go from Here?

Job hunting is complex, chaotic, time-consuming, energy-draining, and really a full eight-hours (or more)-a-day job if we are doing it right.

A letter from a friend who had also experienced job loss touched my heart. He wrote, "I'm sorry that you are currently dealing with some trauma. Believe me, I know how you feel. I've been there."

Additional statements amplified on the circumstances surrounding his traumatic leave-taking from where he had been employed for some time. "It took me three years to work through my feelings," he said. Yes, he understood!

I appreciated the tone of my friend's letter and the integrity it showed. Indeed, he had worked through his anger and his feelings. I benefited immensely from his wise counsel. But three years! That's a long time. *Can it be shortened?* I wondered. What could I do to bounce back from the blow I had received?

A Bounce-Back Guide

I discovered some "survival tactics" that helped me get through my unemployment. Perhaps you're ready to put some of them to work in your own life. I've provided these tactics here in capsulated form, and some are explained in more detail in succeeding chapters.

Confront the Uglies

Resolve the rage. Deal with your anger. Emily Koltnow and Lynne S. Dumas write in *Congratulations! You've Been Fired*: "When you get fired, you're put aboard an emotional stagecoach. In time it will bring you to your ultimate destination: that terrific new position or career. But first, you have to pass through some painful emotional stages that lie in every firing's wake."[1]

Take some time "to recoup emotionally and not beat yourself up for not having the energy to get right out there and charge ahead immediately with finding a job," advises a counselor at the AARP Worker Equity Department.

Depending on the circumstances surrounding your job loss, some strong feelings and words may erupt. Frankly, I'm of the opinion that we don't need to feel guilty when this happens. It's important to allow those angry feelings a way of escape. Maybe someone else sabotaged your job or you think about all the time and energy you invested in the company and your position . . . and now this!

"Payday someday," I told a friend who also expressed anger.

"But when?" she cried out.

"Carol, it's up to God," I responded. "My part is not to allow this anger to overpower me. I have to rein it in even though it's important I get it out."

If verbalizing your feelings helps you to rid yourself of anger's possible poisoning effects, then I urge you to vent your feelings. But in the process, try to laugh at the idiocy of what has happened to you. *Idiocy* is a good word to describe the injustices that are often foisted upon hardworking, innocent people who lose their jobs. Get your situation in perspective and you won't feel so bad about yourself. This leads to another strategy for survival fitness.

Hang On to Your Sense of Humor

Becoming austere about what has taken place and wiping out all the fun in our lives won't improve our chances of getting the job we want. Searching for a job is serious business, no doubt about it. Our livelihoods have been lost, if not our identities. But a very important part of our state of mind and job-search attitude must be laughter and some play. As author Tim Hansel says, "Pain is inevitable, but misery is optional."

Best-selling author Barbara Johnson often uses Hansel's quote, wisely pointing out that the only thing you can really control in this life is your own mental attitude. Barb didn't lose a job; she lost two sons—one was killed in Vietnam, the other by a drunken driver. Her third son informed her that he had chosen a homosexual lifestyle. (He eventually left that lifestyle, but not before my friend went through an incredible amount of trauma and pain.)

"It's no fun to suffer; in fact, it can be awful," she says, "regardless of what has caused that suffering. But we can decide how we will react to the pain that inevitably comes to us all. The most important thing I learned is that having a proper mental attitude works wonders. If you take care of yourself and do all the things that you must do to keep it in control so that it doesn't control you, you can live a happy, productive life."[2]

Barb says a good cry is a wet-wash, but a hearty laugh gives you a good dry cleaning. And a good laugh is worth a hundred groans any time in any market. When you laugh in spite of the circumstances that surround you, you will enrich others, enrich yourself, and, more than that, you will *last*! The wisdom writer knew what he was talking about when he wrote, "A merry heart doeth good like a medicine" (Prov. 17:22 KJV).

Barbara advises, "Life isn't always what you want, but it's what you've got; so, with God's help, choose to be happy." Everything I've read emphasizes the need to remain positive, to maintain a good attitude, and not to cave in to negativism. While this isn't implying that we must always be bubbly and perky, it does require that we determine not to succumb to discouragement or despair.

Although we don't make light of serious things, the ability to poke fun at ourselves once in a while can be an attractive trait, and it goes a long way in easing the pain of job loss trauma. Assessing the "why" of job loss early on can be very helpful in coping with accompanying emotional reactions. Very often in assessing what has happened, we are able to see that we have fallen victim to circumstances beyond our control (which is not to say that there aren't instances when one has to share some responsibility for a termination). A sense of humor has a way of reducing people and problems to their proper proportions.

Laughter is jogging on the inside, and we all need to do more of it. Hopefully, someone is helping to put some sparkles in your life. Find something to laugh about, even if it's only going to the card store and getting a kick out of Hallmark's Shoebox cards, which never fail to tickle my funny bone, or some of the other humorous things there. As someone has said, "Laughter is a tranquilizer with no side effects."

Nikki, one of my delightful friends, said upon learning of my job loss, "That creep! He didn't deserve to have you on staff." She and I had worked together at a previous place and had both received our walking papers along with thirty-six others on the same day. She mentioned that incident and the man who had been in charge there, and added, "He was a creep too!" We both laughed. Name calling isn't something my friend and I go around doing, but she was angry too. Sometimes we are justified, and I have a feeling God understands. Jesus himself had a few choice words to express how he felt about the unscrupulous actions of some men he encountered. Both Matthew and Luke record his use of the term "brood of vipers" on more than one occasion. Jesus also called the scribes and Pharisees "hypocrites." He amplified on that, saying they were like whitewashed tombs that appear beautiful outwardly but inside are full of dead men's bones and all uncleanness. Talk about strong words!

Become Proactive

Proactive is a very common word in management literature. Defined, it means that we are responsible for our own lives, that our behavior is a function of our decisions, not our conditions. In practice, it means that we aren't going to blame circumstances, conditions, or conditioning for our behavior; instead, what happens to us is going to be a product of our own conscious choice, based on our values. Someone has said that life is about 10 percent how you make it and 90 percent how you take it.

We can subordinate feelings to values. It is up to us to take the initiative and accept the responsibility to make things happen. We don't have to react to people and circumstances; instead, we can choose to respond according to our internalized values. When we do this, our burdens, whatever they may be, will not paralyze our progress. The truth is that someone may, in fact, have done us wrong. I experienced that, and what happened to me was wrong. We are tempted to do what comes naturally, but the better part of wisdom is to do what comes supernaturally, and that is to forgive and love the person who wronged you.

Stephen Covey says, "Proactive people can carry their own weather with them." In other words, it doesn't make any difference to them whether it's raining or shining.

Decide that you won't be the victim of someone else's decisions as it relates to your job loss. Eleanor Roosevelt observed, "No one can hurt you or make you feel inferior without your consent."

Be Honestly Confrontive with Yourself

I have developed this life principle: I have to live with myself, so I want to be fit for myself to know. Oliver Wendell Holmes wrote, "What lies behind us and what lies before us are tiny matters compared to what lies within us." Instead of waiting for something good to happen, try making it happen for yourself. Today's preparation is tomorrow's achievement.

What if your job loss had something to do with undesirable performance? What if your attitude and demeanor had been unpleasant? What if you hadn't done something right and it had been pointed out to you but you continued to do it "your way"? Would sweeping the truth under the rug and making excuses for yourself help you in the long run? No, it wouldn't.

To be honestly confrontive with oneself requires that you give yourself permission to admit whatever it is that needs admitting *without* beating up on yourself. Trashing and berating yourself for too long will only end up damaging your emotional health. Be honest about what happened and then move on.

It's not so much *what happens* to us, but *our responses to what happens* that ultimately hurts or helps us the most.

If we were responsible for contributing to the decision that brought about our termination, then the better part of wisdom dictates that we do some self-examination. We need to be ruthlessly honest with ourselves and set about to make changes. "You know what?" a man might say to his wife. "I think I really blew it." Just saying something like that helps to let off the steam, because inwardly we may be seething at ourselves. Some wise sage said, "He who finds no fault in himself needs a second opinion."

Not to face the fact that corrective measures may be required is to short-circuit what will work in our favor in the future. To get out of a difficulty, one usually must go through it. I have made some discoveries through these trying times. When I say to myself, "Helen, you can choose to respond in ways that won't add to your problems, or you can respond so that you prolong the agony and make yourself and others around you miserable in the process," I am being honestly confrontive with myself. And doing so is going to work in my favor.

Organize Your Finances

Sudden unemployment is a financial nightmare, and the possibility exists that it will become a financial disaster. Are there ways to minimize the damage?

Start with your outlook. I read about an American team setting out to climb Mount Everest. A psychologist talked to the men individually before they left for Nepal. He asked each one, "Are you going to make it to the top of Everest?" Most, in their own way, answered, "Well, I'm sure going to give it my best shot," or "That's what we're going to try to do." But one man looked quietly at the questioner for a moment and then said, "Yes, I'm going to make it to the top of Everest." And he did. Out of that group, he was the only one to reach the summit.

All of us come face-to-face with Everest-like situations at one time or another. The financial problems that accompany unemployment can loom as insurmountable as Mount Everest. Most people say that, at best, they could survive three months without a paycheck. (Many I talked with, however, say they couldn't make it beyond a month or six weeks at the most.) Prolonged unemployment is financially damaging. "With God's help," I said over and over again, "we are going to survive. We are survivors. We will be winners."

Approach financial planning from the point of view that you may be unemployed longer than anticipated. From the outset you are well advised to hold down expenses that in normal times would not be considered a problem. This includes things such as entertainment expenses, gifts, trips, contributions, unnecessary long-distance telephone calls, magazine subscriptions, new clothes, and dry cleaning. I developed a mind-set that said cut back, cut out, curtail, think twice before spending, and give up what is nonessential.

Notifying creditors if it appears you will fall behind or not be able to pay your bills is important. Some people try to get a consolidation loan, borrowing on their home equity or using other resources as collateral. A number of unemployed people told me they were able to borrow against life insurance policies rather than cashing them in. (Usually such policies offer a low interest rate.) Refinancing one's home and taking advantage of lower interest rates when they occur is wise.

You may find it necessary to sell some assets: a second car, sports equipment (boats, planes, snowmobiles, campers), expensive cameras, jewelry, musical equipment, stamp or coin collections, works of art, unused furniture, paintings, lawn and/or farm equipment, secondary properties.

The unemployed told me they had garage sales or they cashed in on IRAs, savings bonds, stocks, certificates of deposit, or retirement and pension plans. Others sold their homes.

Your financial planning should make allowance for expenses connected with a job search: stamps, resumes, word-processing fees, phone charges, added transportation, and so on. Keep good records of these expenses—they may be tax deductible, depending on your filing status. Consult with a qualified tax preparer.

If generating income is an immediate problem (which it is for most people), look for part-time or evening work, trying, however, to keep some time free for the job search itself.

Invest in Yourself

You may be thinking, *How can she talk about financial problems in one breath and in the next say, "Invest in yourself"?* At the front end of your job search, you may need to spend money for resumes that are word processed and printed on good bond paper unless you can do a really good job on a resume yourself. Some employers provide this service either through actual dollars or by allowing you to use their copy machine.

Other employers provide outplacement counseling as a major severance benefit. In essence, outplacement involves helping to market people into satisfactory new jobs. In some instances, it involves helping the severed employee master skills that can help him or her relocate into another kind of job. Consulting firms and outplacement companies that specialize in this are paid by the company doing the firing. They provide very individualized psychological, analytical, and technical support during the transition period. It's a well-timed development, but not all people are placed nor do all ex-employees receive this.

Whatever is offered to you in the way of severance, use the resources wisely and allot some of it to invest in yourself. This may include retraining, taking classes, or seeing a professional job counselor.

Would You Hire You?

Ask yourself this question: Would you hire you? It may be helpful to write out the reasons why you would or would not. Then take the steps to make whatever changes are called for. Listen to yourself. Examine your attitude. Actively work to improve your outlook. Remember, *you are your own calling card*. Make the right statement. Look sharp! Be sharp!

Praise Energizes

It has been wisely said that there is no putdown quite so devastating as the self-putdown. Howard Figler, in *The Complete Job-Search Handbook*, says self-putdowns stick because we make them stick. We don't want others to think we are egocentric, pompous, or boastful, so we build hedges into every victory or achievement.

In contrast, emphasizes Figler, praise is the precious fuel that propels you to surpass yourself. While you need not depend on the compliments of others or judge yourself by your opinions of you, you must maintain (or regain) the capacity to congratulate yourself.[3]

Pay Attention to Three "Re" Words

We must pay attention to three important "re" words: *retrain*, *relocate*, and *rethink*. This is common-sense thinking; to reestablish one's self in the workplace depends a lot on one's flexibility. Be open-minded and flexible. There are heartening signs for the job market, but a lot may depend on your willingness to become competent in some other line of work or even move to a more prosperous job market.

Throughout my job loss ordeal, I promised myself and our family that I would maintain an open mind. "This may mean relocation," I told them, "and it may mean I move into another field, which would involve some retraining."

The dictionary defines *flexibility* as the ability to bend without breaking; not to be stiff or rigid, but to be pliant. It is closely akin to *resiliency*, and the two in tandem make a strength that provides the assurance that we can recover our spirits and move in a different direction if necessary.

I saw flexibility in my husband some years ago. Following a long and fulfilling musical career, he was confronted with the need for a job change. I reminded him that before going into the music ministry, he had been a school principal. "But I left it," he explained, "because I preferred a career in music." Just saying that helped him to see it was time to bend. Within weeks he was back at work in the field of education for which he was also trained and highly skilled.

Research

There is a whole world of helpful information out there and all you have to do is avail yourself of it. One of the most helpful places you can go is to a public library. If you have colleges or universities in your area, their libraries are very impressive and helpful.

Columnist Joyce Lain Kennedy, who speaks of today's job market as being stagnant and bloated with rising unemployment claims, urges job seekers to rethink their way around obstacles littering the job hunt and go back to following the more traditional recruitment processes that include newspaper ads, job fairs, networking, and library research. She relates that employers' email boxes are jam-packed, and some resumes never get noticed despite the use of sophisticated software designed to snare the most qualified applicants. I report this not to scare you away from using the Internet but to urge you not to limit yourself. Kennedy says, "Go high-touch instead of high-tech."[4]

Of course the Internet continues to yield good leads for the avid researcher, but don't put all your eggs in one basket, as the old saying goes. One man told me he didn't hear from what he thought would be a promising position until a year *after* he'd sent his resume. He had discovered the job listing via the Internet. "Just shows you how overrated the Internet is for landing a job," he told me. He didn't get the job. Thankfully, he hadn't limited his search nor built up his hopes too high. In that intervening year, he was hired by an international firm. How did he get the job? He drove through the industrial parks in his city, taking down the names of companies that he knew used people in his line of work. Then he sent a well-crafted letter to each company stating his interest in what they were doing. The company that eventually hired him contacted him and asked that he send his resume. An interview followed. His diligence paid off handsomely.

Richard Bolles maintains that this kind of investigative work—that is, knocking on the door of any employer, factory, or office that interests you, whether they are known to have a vacancy or not—is one of the five best ways to hunt for a job. It has a 47 percent success rate. That is, out of every one hundred people who use this search method, forty-seven will find a job. Not bad!

Kennedy insists that when recruiting software is slamming online doors in your face, you should shift your emphasis toward tried and proven approaches to the job search that bypass technology. She points to Bolles's JobHuntersBible .com and what he calls for in creative job hunting. I have found Kennedy and Bolles to be *the best* resources for sound advice. The weekend edition of your nearest large city newspaper probably carries Kennedy's column, which provides a wealth of information. Both Bolles's and Kennedy's books are worth the investment, or you can check them out at the library.

Kennedy urges that you review how you have been spending your time since you became unemployed. You may need to remap your job-hunting strategy.

If too many hours have gone to Internet job sites where you're competing with countless competitors for the same jobs, back off and limit Net time to nights and weekends.

The online hiring rate isn't impressive, probably under 8 percent for white- and blue-collar jobs combined. By cutting back, you free up prime time to contact people who can hire you or chat up people who may know about job openings.[5]

You can find more on using the Internet in part 2.

Other sources for information are trade associations, corporations (their newsletters, annual reports, company magazines), the Yellow Pages, City Hall (listings of available jobs area-wide are usually posted; this is largely an unknown and untapped resource center), and your local Chamber of Commerce. Don't forget to watch the business section of area papers to keep abreast of management changes, promotions, and new hires. This is one of the best places to pick up on names of people to whom you could write. Business sections will also alert you to growth opportunities within industries. A vast amount of information can be gleaned from diligent research.

You will also want to visit Internet book sites and local bookstores, such as Borders, Barnes and Noble, and some of the other larger bookstores where you can browse to your heart's content.

"Great discoveries in the occupational mystery can be yours if you accept this challenge," says Kennedy. She recommends that you spend forty-eight hours visually traipsing through business newspaper sections, magazines, and relevant occupational books. When you set out on your research work, equip yourself with a notebook, pens, dimes, and quarters. Many books and pamphlets cannot be checked out of the library, so come prepared to make copies and write down ideas and information.

Watch your local and area-wide newspapers and business journals for information about meetings you can attend aimed specifically at job seekers. While in northern California researching job possibilities, I followed two publications: *Career Currents* and the *California Job Journal*. No doubt you will find such papers available in your part of the country as well. These publications alerted me to job fairs, seminars, and meetings.

You can best stay abreast of openings in your geographic area of interest and in the fields you are trained for by this kind of diligent ongoing research. The Internet can link you to regional job sites, particularly if you are in a metropolitan area. Watch the Sunday editions of newspapers as well.

You may need to hire research assistance. This is virtually imperative for executives and can save most people hundreds of hours of work. Such in-depth assistance can be provided by someone who has access to database information. I turned the corner in my own job search when I finally went for some career counseling and sought the help of a highly recommended gentleman (more on this in part 2) who introduced me to the database computer-generated information I needed.

Other sources of information are available that will not cost you anything other than your time. One of the best-known information sources is the *National Business Employment Weekly* published by the *Wall Street Journal*. Check it out on the Internet or at the library. You may find it on the newsstand. It is also available by subscription.

Conduct a Focused Job Search

When you seriously plunge into the job hunt, you will discover that you must actively pursue a variety of sources. Target the kind of job you want and go for it. To help you do this, I have provided some job-assessment tools and other helpful information in part 2. There you will discover how to write what one managing editor at a company where I applied called my "knock-the-socks-off" resume. You will learn what should go into a cover letter if you hope to capture the attention of decision makers. And again, you will find a vast amount of help the Internet can provide.

You will be shown the importance of networking, publicizing your job search, and marketing yourself. There are ideas on where to look for unadvertised jobs and how to handle newspaper ads. I'll inform you about registering with placement agencies and tell you how to ace the interview by leading with your strengths. Many other things are covered that will help you land a job you can love.

Losing Your Job Can Lead to Better Things

A woman who was laid off spoke of the light-headed and nauseous feelings she had. "Forget thirteen years of working day and night," she said. "Forget being rated one of the top ten producers in the state. None of that mattered. I got the ax because of politics, pure and simple. And while I stood there thinking, *This just can't be happening to me*, he had the audacity to tell me not to take it personally.

"The only thing I remember after that is putting on a happy face, going home, and crying for the next two days. By the third day I'd had enough of that." She describes waking up angrier than she'd ever been in her life and vowing she was never going to let that happen to her again.

She also learned not to let the experience destroy her self-worth. "Like most people, I had tied my self-worth to my job," she explained, "so when I got laid off, I thought I wasn't worth anything. It took me a while to realize that I was fine. I'd just been had by the system because I had left myself wide open."

How had she done this? "I really believed all that stuff about being loyal and doing a good job and the company taking care of you. Wrong!" she fairly shouted. "It really doesn't matter how good you are; everyone's dispensable. And it's usually the people who aren't as good that stay or get promoted. I finally realized that I'm good, and they're the losers."

Did I ever identify with that woman's statements! But let's reckon with this, even as she did: We aren't powerless. We don't have to keep on getting clobbered by things we don't have any control over. This woman decided to start her own company—something many unemployed people end up doing. She printed up a batch of business cards, started calling everybody she knew, and began pulling in clients for her services. It worked. Today she says she's making more money than she did before, and she's having more fun. A great ending to a sad beginning!

This can be your story. Being laid off can be one of the best things that ever happens to you. This woman admitted, "I never fully realized that until it was all over and my life was a lot more like I wanted it to be. Funny, somehow it feels like I got pushed off a cliff and learned I could fly."

Here's What Can Be Done

The one thing over which we have control is ourselves. Let's acknowledge our mistakes where they exist and work at correcting them. Let's learn from the past, allow it to be a good teacher, and benefit from what we have learned. Let's get to work on ourselves. Let's do what I have previously referred to as the near-at-hand things to bring order and stability into our lives, and then trust God to do for us what we cannot do for ourselves. This was the guiding principle that worked for me, and I repeat it here to underscore how important it is.

Richard Bolles wrote to me in a personal letter during the height of my job-loss trauma, "You are on the right track, praying as though everything depends on God, and working as though everything depends on you." That is at the very heart of surviving sudden unemployment. He really encouraged me.

> Trust in the LORD with all your heart,
> And lean not on your own understanding;
> In all your ways acknowledge Him,
> And He shall direct your paths.

> Proverbs 3:5–6

6

Chasing
the Pink-Slip Blues

The first thing that crosses our minds after becoming suddenly unemployed is the need to do whatever it takes to find
another job. Now, after many months of rethinking what
job loss is all about, I recognize that the immediate need
was, and is, the right mind-set.

If a person is planning to run a marathon, he or she doesn't
wait until the last minute to prepare. Months of rigor-
ous preparation and training precede a race. Likewise, a
job search requires that we be mentally, emotionally, and
physically fit to perform at our best throughout the search.
We do not think with clarity when our emotional state is
less than it should be. We can easily lose our competitive
edge when our unhappiness, anger, and anxiety are appar-
ent. Judith Dubin and Melanie Keveles write in *Fired for
Success*, "Our experience with thousands of successful job
searchers who had been fired is that the person who has let

go of his anger and unhappiness about having been fired is the one who conducts the best job search."[1]

In responding to a letter I'd written, a trusted friend told me in no uncertain terms that I was ax-grinding. He had detected some anger, and rightly so. I was angry, and more than any other emotional reaction, this was where I waged my hardest battle. My situation was compounded by the fact that I had been wrongfully discharged, and so, as I was repeatedly told, my anger was justified. Nevertheless, I had to get over it, and with prayer and the wise counseling of my husband, I was able to do so. When wrenching changes come into our lives, coming to terms with what has happened is always painful and stressful. How can we get our emotions under control and maintain our balance? Are there some things we can do to protect ourselves from the devastating effects of our situation? What will help us put everything in perspective?

The Five Stages of Loss

In Elisabeth Kübler-Ross's landmark study of death and dying, she speaks of the five stages of loss.[2] You are likely familiar with her findings, but they are worth noting here: (1) denial and isolation, (2) anger, (3) bargaining, (4) depression, and (5) acceptance.

These stages can vary in intensity and duration, but most of us go through all of them when we lose a job. Sometimes we become stuck in one stage far too long, and that can cause enormous problems.

Denial and Isolation

On the day I was let go, I came to work expecting business as usual. My "to do" list showed several projects under way and some approaching deadlines. I worked steadily all day and at 4:30 shut off the computer, stretched, and glanced out the window. Just then the phone rang. I was summoned into my immediate superior's office, where the office manager was sitting as well.

"Do you have something to tell us?" one asked. The other fidgeted nervously.

"No . . . no. What do you mean?"

"You asked for a few days off . . ."

The air was electric. "Yes, it felt great to get away. I told you I was exhausted after working all those months on ghosting that book." I explained that we had driven south to see my husband's ninety-six-year-old aunt in a rest home. She had been asking for us. "Is anything wrong?"

"Yes, Dr. ___ doesn't believe you. He thinks you were looking for another job. You're fired. You have a half hour to clear the things out of your office."

Numb, dazed, disoriented—through the haze I heard "severe financial problems . . . we'll be selling some of the TV stations . . . other terminations, you are the first of many . . ."

Somehow I walked out of that office. My mind was reeling with a "this really isn't happening to me" feeling.

The immediate reaction when loss occurs is denial: *This can't be happening to me. I don't believe this. I had no idea. No, not me; it can't be true.* We actually go into a state of shock. As Koltnow and Dumas explain, "Shock is your psyche's way of cushioning the blow." Denial acts as a buffer after unexpected shocking news. It allows a person time to collect himself or herself and, with time, mobilize other, less radical defenses.

Denial is a temporary defense, so you can expect other emotional reactions to replace it eventually. These initial feelings of denial may be accompanied by some sustained feelings of numbness. As they disappear and you begin to collect yourself, you may have a desire to retreat into some form of isolation. You just want to get away from your situation, so you withdraw from everybody and everything.

Surprisingly, you may find yourself isolated from others who don't know how to handle your problem and therefore avoid you. Job loss can cause alienation in relationships, especially with former co-workers. They may fear for their own jobs and may even have been threatened with job loss themselves if they have anything to do with you. Two former co-workers told me they had been warned in this manner.

Those who get stuck in the denial stage often respond inappropriately and even cheerfully when confronted with job loss. Be patient and understanding. Reality has a way of eventually pulling us back to our senses.

Anger

According to Kübler-Ross, when the first stage of denial can't be maintained any longer, it is replaced by feelings of anger, rage, envy, and resentment. I was totally unprepared for the anger I felt.

Your family and friends may find it very difficult to cope with this stage. I was fortunate that my husband handled it with compassion and understanding. "It's not irrational anger," he explained to me time after time. "You were lied to. No one else has been terminated as they said would happen. None of their assets have been sold. In fact, they've bought two more TV stations . . ." He talked it out with me each time the anger reared its ugly head, helping me to better understand my rage.

Those of us who have lost our jobs need to realize that our husbands or wives are also feeling wounded and anxious. One morning I sensed that my husband was disturbed. He slammed two cupboard doors, the bathroom door, and the door leading to the basement all within a few minutes of each other. He wasn't upset with me. His own anger was surfacing, and this was his way of getting rid of it.

Sometimes family members become targets of our anger. This helps to explain why so many individuals experience disruptions in their relationships as a result of trauma and loss. We may be short-tempered and hostile. We may have temper tantrums and complain or get into unnecessary arguments. We likely will raise our voices or make demands and threats.

If you're the innocent bystander, what can you do? Don't take it personally. If you do and respond in kind, it will feed into the person's already hostile behavior. My husband used different approaches to ease me through the angry outbursts. He'd take me for a ride, a walk through the mall, or a visit to the library. Sometimes he'd make arrangements for us to get together with friends. Often he would say, "Come here; let's pray." At other times, he'd wrap me in his arms and say, "Here, dear, this is meant just for you," and he'd hand an open Bible to me, pointing to a verse or passage. And always he kept beautiful music going throughout the house.

When I lost my job, I retreated to my computer that night and began writing out my feelings. Writing is very therapeutic for me. Whatever is therapeutic for you, get into it and enjoy it. If it's golfing, get out there with friends and tee off. You will be doing more than swinging at a ball!

When I finished the first draft of this book some months later, I asked a friend to read it. Usually I don't do that, but in my heart I suspected there were some raw edges that hadn't been dealt with. I knew my husband would find it difficult to be objective; he was too close to what had happened. I knew the person I asked to read it, a college professor (he and his wife are dearest friends), was wise enough to be kindly honest with me. He was. He attached little yellow notes throughout (they were appreciated, Orrin), and one of them said, "You still haven't fully dealt with your anger." *Groan!* But he was right. This version of the book bears little resemblance to the original!

My anger was prolonged more than either my husband or I expected. We decided to try harder to understand why. At some point it occurred to us that this was, in part, righteous anger. I hadn't become bitter, though that danger always exists (and the Bible cautions about allowing this to happen). And I wasn't wanting revenge. This anger was something more—something beyond us. We came to see it as the kind of anger Jesus experienced when he overthrew the tables of those who bought and sold in the temple (see Matt. 21:12; Mark 11:15).

Clearly, the Holy Spirit in me was roused to indignation. I can tell you this in good conscience because I had worked very, very hard at my job. Much had been accomplished to reshape the image of the organization—something I was specifically hired to do. I was told by a former co-worker that a few weeks after I was gone, some work had fallen behind and was not up to the expectations of the founder. In a meeting, the founder said, "If Helen were here, this wouldn't have happened . . ." and then caught himself, realizing what had just escaped his lips. Well, okay, so it sounds like I'm bragging, but it did happen.

Lee Iacocca, in writing about getting fired, spoke of the anger and humiliation he experienced: "I began my life as the son of immigrants, and I worked my way up to the presidency of the Ford Motor Company. When I finally got there, I was on top of the world. But then fate said to me: 'Wait. We're not finished with you. Now you're going to find out what it feels like to get kicked off Mt. Everest!'"

Iacocca had been president of Ford for eight years and a Ford employee for thirty-two. "On July 13, 1978, I was fired. . . . I had never worked anywhere else. And now, suddenly, I was out of a job. It was gut-wrenching." His anger was strong, especially as he considered what his job loss was doing to his wife and two daughters: "They were the innocent victims of the despot whose name was on the building."

Three months later Iacocca went to Chrysler—a move he described as jumping from the frying pan into the fire. A year later Chrysler came within a whisker of bankruptcy.

"Being fired at Ford was bad enough. But going down with the ship at Chrysler was more than I deserved."

Iacocca talks about the thousands of little forks in the road and a few really big forks—those moments of reckoning, moments of truth. This was his experience as he wondered what to do: "Should I pack it all in and retire?" he asked of himself. He was fifty-four years old, had already accomplished a great deal, and was financially secure. He could afford to play golf for the rest of his life. "But that just didn't feel right," he said. "I knew I had to pick up the pieces and carry on. There are times in everyone's life when something constructive is born out of adversity. There are times when things seem so bad that you've got to grab your fate by the shoulder and shake it."

He spoke of the private pain as being something he could have endured, but the deliberate public humiliation was too much. "I was full of anger, and I had a simple choice: I could turn that anger against myself, with disastrous results. Or I could take some of that energy and try to do something productive."

In times of great stress and adversity, it's always best to keep busy, to plow your energy into something positive, Iacocca urges.[3]

Dubin and Keveles warn that if you are fired, the tendency is to dwell on such things as what you may have done wrong, how you should have anticipated what happened, what you could have done differently, or whether you were treated worse than others. This can become a vicious cycle, taking up too much mental "space," preventing you from focusing on what you are moving toward. Even though you may need to explore what happened to make sure you don't duplicate the situation and even if you have not resolved in your own mind whose "fault" it was or exactly what happened to contribute to your demise, it is important to move on.[4]

I have outlined below ten steps for releasing angry feelings that worked for me. Hopefully, working through these steps will help you regain your equilibrium and enable you to move on.

Working through Your Angry Feelings

1. Permit yourself to feel the feelings that you feel. Acknowledge them. Refrain from telling yourself you shouldn't have such feelings.
2. Understand that feelings are an energy force and, as such, must be accepted. To repress your feelings as if they don't exist is tantamount to attacking other vital forces, such as the very act of breathing. Just as you need to breathe, you need to feel.
3. Anger isn't going to go away because you or someone else attempts to shame yourself. Anger will dissipate after we express it, allow ourselves to hear it, deal with it, and release it.
4. Recognize that anger is part of the grieving process—one of the five stages of loss as defined by Kübler-Ross. Grieving requires time to complete the process.
5. Giving appropriate expression to your job loss is a means of releasing your hurt feelings. Think through the process as you feel your feelings. This will give God room to move upon your heart, opening up wonderful possibilities for present peace and future good.
6. Try laughing at yourself. Humor always helps release the pain. Someone has said that you can tell that you have come to terms with an issue when you can see humor through the seriousness.
7. Be willing to accept feedback from others whose counsel and judgment you respect.
8. Pay attention to your gut feelings. As my career counselor said to me, "Your gut feelings are generally very reliable. If something someone says or does makes you 'sick to your stomach,' that's probably not advice you should heed."

9. Your negative, angry feelings may be displaying themselves to other people, including job interviewers. You must deal with them, or they will hurt your chances of being hired. A positive, sunny disposition with as much optimism as you can muster will be one of the best assets you have in job hunting. Interviewers will respect you for this.

10. Nothing interferes with and/or destroys inner peace as much as anger, whether it's wildly fuming or slowly simmering. Focus your thoughts on God. Call upon him for the help he is ready to provide: "You will keep him in perfect peace, whose mind is stayed on You, because he trusts in You. Trust in the LORD forever" (Isa. 26:3).

Bargaining

This stage is not something most of us who experience job loss go through to any great degree. Most bargaining is an attempt to get God to change his mind about the events in our lives. It has a lot to do with fear and excessive guilt over real or perceived past behavior.

Depression

Depression is related to a sense of loss, and that's what we have experienced. We have lost our jobs. Our security is at stake. And that's scary. Sometimes unrealistic guilt can accompany such depression. Most often it is unwarranted. We may experience sorrow, anguish, and anxiety as well. These are normal emotions arising out of the enormity of what has happened to us. Reality slaps us in the face; we feel the sting and are confronted with a sense of hopelessness.

We may find that our attempts to find work aren't getting the job done. We begin to question our value and expertise. Self-doubt, self-blame, and humiliation enter into

91

our thoughts unbidden. We start coming down hard on ourselves. In reality, rarely does failure to find a job have anything to do with who we are. It does have a lot to do with the number of people applying for the same jobs we are seeking.

Over and over I heard, "You won't believe how many people have responded to the ad." One human resource manager told me she had more than fifteen hundred resumes to sort through. In letters and private conversations with human resource managers, I heard the same thing. Sometimes during the interview process, the person would point to his desk and say, "See that stack? That's the resumes that have come in for this position." I felt fortunate to have made it to the top of such stacks. When I began to understand what was happening, my depression lifted considerably.

Here's what I learned: the key for me in overcoming discouragement and depression was to keep my thinking in tune with scriptural truths. I knew from past experiences that only when the principles of the Word, and *not* my emotions or moods, dictated my responses could I make responsible choices.

Moreover, I know who my enemy is, and he is your enemy too. When the apostle Peter told us we have an enemy who goes about like a roaring lion, seeking whom he may devour, he wasn't kidding. "Resist him," Peter urged, "steadfast in the faith" (1 Pet. 5:8–9). If that lion is roaring in your ears right now, and you want to rout him, you must take the step that will move you out of lion country. "Get thee behind me, Satan," works for me—five simple words that Jesus used. Know for certain that any depression you experience as a result of your job loss is the devil trying to do a number on you. Fight him. Fight hard. God takes no pleasure in seeing his children hurt and victimized. You can trust God to vindicate you in his time. Let him fight your battles for you. Draw on his strength and move on. You will come out a winner.

Acceptance

Contrary to what people think, acceptance is not necessarily a happy stage. Sometimes it is void of feelings. But when reached, this point allows you to once again step out with dignity and serenity.

As I said to a friend, if my happiness was dependent on circumstances, I'd have bowed out of the scene a long time ago. Such happiness can be very fleeting. Your house can go up in smoke, your new car can be demolished, and yes, your job can go down the drain. The joy of the Lord is deeper than happiness. Joy is the strength he supplies in our crisis times. To depend on him is never misplaced dependence.

Yet even when we have reached the acceptance stage, we may still be bothered by some embarrassment. I found this to be true. A friend inquired about my job loss and then raised his eyebrows when he was told the truth. (Talk about the effects of body language!) To myself I was thinking, *Guess I should have lied and said I quit.* But it was a fleeting thought. For some of us, lying isn't even an option. No, I couldn't and wouldn't lie.

If you are at all intuitive, you will spot those who don't believe you. Some people will think you brought your job loss on yourself. Whether intentionally or inadvertently, people sometimes do "burst our bubbles." How can you handle it? Acceptance. In acceptance lieth peace.

Horace Greeley said, "Fame is a vapor; popularity an accident. Riches take wing; those who cheer today will curse tomorrow; only one thing endures—character." Character that has its roots grounded in the love and teachings of the Bible will stand up though the winds of adversity blow hard.

Let your life be a statement, more than your words, that someone else is in charge. Let your demeanor reflect inner control and stability that comes from knowing and accepting that God is in charge. In time—in God's perfect timing—wrongs will be righted, things will change, and he will come to your rescue. To believe this is to move on and live with hope. As Job said in his time of trial, "[God] knows the way that I take; when He has tested me, I shall come forth as gold" (Job 23:10).

Be Good to Yourself

Studies have been done on the effects of job loss that show conclusively that getting fired can be harmful to your health. Harvey Brenner, professor of behavioral sciences at Johns Hopkins University, has found a statistically significant relationship between job loss and mortality from cardiovascular and renal disease, cirrhosis of the liver (often brought about by excessive drinking), and even suicide.

The idea that stress is bad for your health is nothing new. Stress tends to weaken the body's resistance to germs. Scientists at the Medical Research Council Common Cold Unit in Salisbury, England, reported some interesting findings on volunteers who had been exposed to cold viruses. The researchers calculated a numerical stress level for each volunteer by questioning him or her about such burdensome events as job loss, ended relationships, moving, sickness, death in the family, and pressure from life's challenges. They discovered that the more stress people had in their lives the more likely they were to catch cold. These findings were reported in the *New England Journal of Medicine*.[5]

Several other health problems can manifest as a result of undue stress, including insomnia, headaches, high blood pressure, and stomach problems. Several women confided in me that after their job loss they put on weight because they couldn't control their binging. Each recognized that she used eating as a way of compensating for what had happened.

Are you struggling with overeating, smoking, alcohol, too much caffeine, drug usage? Be honest. You only hurt yourself (and others who love you) when you refuse to confront whatever it is that is victimizing you.

Taking care of one's health is always important, but never more so than when we are subjected to the kind of stress that accompanies job loss. Common sense tells us that good nutrition and adequate rest protect against stress. Seeking to override emotional concerns alleviates trouble-causing stress factors. Laughter is a stress reducer, and so is exercise. We need to be operating at peak efficiency. To be without a job is bad enough; to find yourself emotionally drained and physically hurting complicates the situation.

Since the first edition of this book was written, I have lost my husband. One of the things I have learned to do is to be good to myself. As I said before, I have to live with myself, and so I need to be fit for myself to know. No longer is my husband around to pat me on the shoulder, whisper encouraging words in my ear, or take me out for lunch or dinner. So now when I sense that I need a change of pace, I take myself out—perhaps it's just a cup of coffee at Starbucks or lunch at a local restaurant, but it's a perker-upper. I suggest that you be good to yourself now and then like this; you deserve it.

Fight or Flight?

We can't get rid of stress. In one way or another, we are surrounded by stress-producing situations, some more devastating and traumatic than others. When severe stress strikes, the body is quickly going to deplete its stores of available nutrients. If we don't replenish these stores, our bodies will not be able to withstand the onslaught, and disease and/or breakdown of body systems will result.

Because I was aware of the damaging effects of prolonged stress, having written a book on the subject for a well-known Southern California nutritionist, I immediately took charge of my situation.[6] With God's help, I told my husband, family, and friends that I would no longer be victimized by the distressing circumstances.

You can do that too. Fortify yourself with extra nutrients that are known to increase the body's resistance against stress-causing wear and tear. The stress of modern life is probably the greatest contributing factor in today's killer diseases, but you can ward off the effects of these stressors. I urge you to acquaint yourself with books and materials that address this subject. You must take charge of your health. Don't expect anyone else to do that for you.

Taking the Bible's Advice

The Bible is very specific in telling us how and how not to handle our emotions. We are emotional beings. Some emotions and attitudes, however, can be disease-producing— things like lovelessness, impatience, unkindness, jealousy, envy, pride, and arrogance; being short-tempered, irritable, grudging, and distrustful; having a get-even attitude and withholding forgiveness when we are wronged.

As to the harmful effects of uncontrolled anger, the biblical warnings are very clear (see Job 5:2; Matt. 5:24; Rom. 12:19; Eph. 4:26–27). Anger may cause us to contemplate doing totally irrational things. Handling rage inappropriately can result in suffering physical and emotional consequences.

The baser side of human nature can show itself in those who may have wronged us or caused us job loss, and it can also show itself in us. With God's help, we can rise above it. The antidote to disease- and stress-producing emotions can be found in such places as Ephesians 4:32, where we are told to be kind, tenderhearted, and forgiving of one another. Forgiveness empowers us. When we take a deep look at our own proclivity to sin and seriously seek to assess our situation, we are equipped by the Holy Spirit for a continuing act of forgiveness. We cannot only forgive ourselves for real or imagined shortcomings, but also those who had to make the hard choice about our employment or dismissal. This is not a once-only thing, but an ongoing necessity.

Empowerment to Sustain Us

God will equip and empower us with what we need to be the kind of men and women who can handle the disturbing events that invade our lives. In many ways, the Bible tells us to make every effort to live in peace with others so that we won't miss the grace of God. We are to prevent the bitter roots of anger, resentment, rancor, and hatred from growing, which can cause terrible trouble and, in fact, defile us (see Heb. 12:15).

We are to center our lives on timeless, unchanging biblical principles that will create in us a fundamental paradigm for effective living. Simply put, we are to stop to think before acting or reacting, allowing the Holy Spirit time to show us the way he wants us to respond. These biblical principles will be validated by the experiences in our lives as we embrace them.

Hopefully, you will implement into your life what you have learned in this chapter. Dubin and Keveles report that in all the clients they have seen through the years, the subtle, intangible quality of a good mental attitude is what makes the difference. It determines the ability of people to recover from the loss of their job, find a career direction, and eventually land a job that is suited to them. Those who are mentally and physically prepared are ready to seriously focus on the rudiments of a good job search.[7]

7

The Age Factor

What happens when you are approaching or are already at "retirement age," but can't afford to retire?

I enjoyed an article that appeared in *USA Today* some years ago telling about the hundred-year-old North Carolinian eye doctor who ran for Congress. Henry Stenhouse said he figured time was on his side. He called his two opponents "capable" but added, "They don't have the advantage I have."

"What's that?" he was asked.

Promptly he replied, "Perspective."

He had five children, fifteen grandchildren, and eighteen great-grandchildren, some of whom even switched parties to vote for him.

Age wasn't an issue, according to the media report. "Everybody loves the old man, so if anybody raised it, they'd be shooting themselves in the foot," said his county Republican Party chairman. Mr. Stenhouse vowed not to serve more than two terms. "I don't want to be there all my life," he reasoned.

When I read this, I applauded Mr. Stenhouse and others like him who continued to make valuable contributions no matter what their age. Yet something perplexes me. As a society we tend to accept politicians, Supreme Court justices, heads of state, and others in such positions of authority who are older, mature, and experienced. Yet that same degree of acceptance is not always extended to the "older" worker in the marketplace and world of work. Evidence the "golden parachutes," the "velvet-covered fists," the "windows," or whatever other name you want to attach to it when "older" workers are eased out of their jobs.

Society has a way of affixing nice-sounding euphemisms to early retirement. But plain and simple, what it really comes down to is getting the ax, often when a person feels she has just hit her stride and is in her prime. I was talking to a real estate agent in Dallas on the phone who, upon learning I was writing a book on being suddenly unemployed, gasped. "What do I say to my husband?" she asked. "How am I supposed to handle his termination? He's devastated. He's only fifty-five, and he's not ready for this. I don't know what to do, what to say. He was making a six-figure salary, but we aren't ready for retirement, neither one of us.

"In fact," she continued, "I'm five years older than he is, but I expect to work until I drop dead. I love working, and so does he."

"Happy Birthday to You . . ."

One day I received a long-distance call. The conversation went like this:

"Helen, this is Eddie."

"What a pleasant surprise! It's been a while. I was going to call and wish you a happy birthday."

"Thanks. Guess what?"

"Hmm. I don't know. You received something special from Don for your birthday."

"Not from Don. But I did receive a surprise. I lost my job today."

"Oh no! I don't believe it. You've been there . . . how long?"

"Almost fourteen years."

"This is too much. What a shock!"

"I'm really in shock, but I'm beginning to better understand what happened to you . . ."

My friend had been asked to train a man for a month and a half to take over her position—a man, by the way, who was much younger than she was. While doing that, she watched what was happening in the company. She saw men and women with seniority like her picking up the company's early retirement buyout and losing their jobs right and left. But she wasn't ready to retire.

She wasn't sure what she should do until she discovered a position within the company where she knew she could work. It wasn't a job the company offered to her; she had only been offered her severance package, which wouldn't have taken care of her needs.

"It's no wonder they didn't offer the job to me," she explained. "It required that I take a 40 percent cut in pay. They were too embarrassed to even let me know about it. But a job is a job, a paycheck is a paycheck. I wasn't too proud to apply for it, and they allowed me to have it."

Eddie was fortunate. Many companies wouldn't do that. When they want "older" employees out the door, that's what they mean and want.

"Velvet-Covered Fists"

Some have termed the corporate practice of getting employees to quit as the "velvet-covered fist." As enticing as the offer may be (especially after a hard day at the office), being asked to quit is nothing short of having a fist shoved in your face. It is "maddeningly complicated," according to *Changing Times* magazine.[1]

"Windows"

The phrase "windows of opportunity" usually suggests something good. The term "windows" was borrowed from companies such as Chrysler, Digital Equipment, IBM, and Kodak, along with *many* others who trimmed tens of thousands from their ranks with what they considered generous cash incentives—*windows* through which older employees could pass into early retirement.

Changing Times spoke of "Big Blue" (IBM) and others who cut their payrolls through such employee buyouts as using "bribes." They explained that such offers flourished in the 1980s and were favored primarily by big corporations with deep pockets. But with the softening in today's economy and the increase in foreign competition, more and more companies are embracing this method of streamlining.[2]

Such buyouts generally target middle managers or veteran production workers with higher salaries. But according to AARP, these buyouts are being misused to rid companies of older employees.

"Golden Parachutes"

Golden parachutes are cash and benefit packages paid to top executives as compensation for losing their jobs if the firm is involved in a merger or a takeover. It is not unusual for some of these chairpersons and CEOs to walk off with several million dollars while shareholders are left shocked with quarterly dividends slashed as much as half or more.

Corporate greed has been rampant for decades in companies governed by greedy top executives, thus accounting for many of the problems that eventually caught up with them.

Severance

When a company tells an employee to clean out his locker or desk, he rarely walks out the door penniless. Usually he receives a final severance check. If part of that check represents pension savings, financial experts caution that the recipient will take a big loss if he spends it all. Since those savings represent years of patient tax deferral that can never be recovered, he will need to carefully assess what to do with it. For instance, if he puts the money into his bank account, he will owe income taxes on the full sum, be liable for a tax penalty, and, if under age fifty-nine and a half, lose the opportunity to make that money continue growing tax deferred.

Financial expert Jane Bryant Quinn says that when you lose your job, you should draw up a bare-bones budget—mortgage, rent, utilities, insurance, car loan, food, gasoline, job-hunting costs. Pay only for these. It is important, however, to tell your other creditors—including credit card companies—that you will send them good-faith checks of ten dollars per month until you are employed again. This should buy you at least six months.

How do you cover the bare-bones budget? If your spouse works and has earnings, you can breathe a little easier. If you have other earnings, unemployment pay, or some savings, turn it into cash to live on. That could include bank accounts, mutual funds, and that portion of your company's good-bye check that doesn't represent retirement money (e.g., severance and vacation pay).

Feeling the Pinch

The climate for a rise in age discrimination is here. When companies face a crumbling economy, they downsize workforces to cut costs. Older workers are particularly vulnerable. Today's lawyers are reporting a surge of people age forty and over seeking help with age-discrimination complaints. Imagine that—forty years old! They cite takeovers where new managers move to bring in their own people. Some companies exhibit a gross insensitivity and arrogance about these cutbacks. They also hire fresh-out-of-college graduates at a far lower salary than the worker with valuable experience. This is deeply disturbing. I personally know individuals who have had this happen to them.

A manager of AARP's Worker Equity advocacy program says they receive hundreds of inquiries per week from people who complain because they have lost jobs, been forced into retirement, or not been hired because of age.

AARP itself is working to educate older workers about age-bias laws. The 1967 Age Discrimination in Employment Act (ADEA), the Older Worker's Benefit Protection Act enacted in October 1990, and state and local statutes protect most people age forty and older against age discrimination in hiring, firing, training, promotion, and benefits. Even so, AARP points out, this hasn't stopped unfair targeting of older employees for layoffs and early retirement "offers" that may be less than voluntary. Write and/or call AARP for information. Look them up on the Internet.

The "Overqualified" Syndrome

Joyce Lain Kennedy says a seasoned mind is too precious to waste. Even the government's *Occupational Outlook Handbook* reports that workers in their mid-thirties to mid-fifties usually have substantial work experience and tend to be stabler and more reliable than younger workers, resulting in higher productivity. Experience really matters, so don't succumb to anyone or anything that tries to imply otherwise!

Still, that leaves a whole army of "seasoned minds" and "stable and reliable people" out there unaccounted for. Their brains haven't ceased functioning. They may have some silver hair now, but that has nothing to do with the capacity of their minds nor the wisdom they have accrued from life experiences.

The employment "game" has changed even within the last decade as many mature workers have discovered. At this point they probably have the credentials that qualify them for the position for which they are applying. They have kept their noses to the proverbial grindstone for years. They have been loyal and have an admirable track record. Kennedy says it strikes a blow to one's dignity to have to "audition," as it were, as he or she did years ago when starting out. Why can't these seasoned workers just land that perfect job? Why do they receive replies to resumes commending them on their impressive qualifications, past experience, and so on, and then hear that they are "overqualified"? How can they get past that?

Being labeled "overqualified" may be accurate in some instances. I applied for positions that I probably could have handled with my eyes closed. When we become desperate, we do end up lowering our expectations.

Understandably, a company isn't going to hire someone who is obviously overqualified. If they do, they will spend time and money acclimating an employee to the job only to have her leave when something more to her liking and more in line with her skills and achievements comes along.

However, as human resource managers look at resumes, they start computing. And what they conclude may relate more to the overage syndrome than it does to being over-qualified. Never mention your age on a resume, and use wisdom in emphasizing work experience that goes back too far. Some books suggest ten years as a minimum, but I consider that unrealistic. (See chapter 10 for what to include and what not to include in your resume.)

Some consultants believe that a letter is more important than a resume for the senior applicant. Information in letters can be more easily slanted to cover experience without giving indication of dates. What you need to do is get your foot in the door for an interview. Once interviewers meet you and see the way you present yourself, they will gain an appreciation for who you are and the good judgment, wisdom, and discernment you possess. Then if they ask about dates, you can be honest without running the risk of being disqualified automatically because of what appears on your resume. In your cover letter, you will want to stress your sound business judgment and provide capsulated statements demonstrating it. Companies are interested in what you can do *for them*. (See suggestions in part 2.)

Kennedy's advice to the mature worker: rearm and re-group. You may have been a star and earned your status, "but in the cutthroat job market of today, you'll need the determination and push you had at twenty-five." She refers to a fired fifty-three-year-old reader who wrote: "I would love to be able to retire from the workforce and just enjoy life, but unfortunately, I'm too young to retire, too old to be useful anymore, and too broke to even consider putting up my feet. So in desperation, I continue to send out resumes." Kennedy's response: "Employers can smell a lack of fire in the belly and stay away in droves."[3]

Even though older workers usually have less absenteeism and less sickness, and are more productive, some companies still think twice before hiring the more mature candidate. Bias against older workers is real, but don't come down too hard on yourself. Some companies and organizations do value the experience and the credibility that a mature worker brings to the job.

Never regard your age and valuable experience as a liability. A sixty-four-year-old vice president of a major international corporation who was without work for seven months told me he feels that his mind has never been sharper and more focused, and that he is in better physical shape now than he has ever been in his life.

Project High Energy

More than anything, what prospective employers are looking for in a mature person is someone who projects a high energy level. The first impression a job hunter makes is always of critical importance. You have no doubt heard the old adage "You never get a second chance to make a first impression." The first five minutes of an interview are frequently more significant than all the rest of the time combined. Project enthusiasm and energy. Project what you are—a tough-minded optimist with an upbeat outlook, regardless of your age.

I had a breakfast meeting at an elegant hotel restaurant with a young businessman, one of three partners in a marketing firm. Two hours later we both looked at our watches and exclaimed our surprise. "I can't believe it," he said. "This has been so much fun!"

Yes, *fun*. The outcome of that interview was that out of the scores of resumes they received, I was their choice. But because they'd had a downturn and didn't receive a major contract they had anticipated, they decided not to hire at the time. "Would you freelance for us," he asked, "until we can bring you on board?" There were three young, aggressive, smart, with-it partners in that firm. I felt good about that, and I did freelance for them.

On another occasion I met with a younger man who was doing the interviewing for a classy private school position for which I was well-qualified. Ten days later he called to say, "I am so disappointed. The woman you and I would be working with put your resume on the top of the stack of those we screened. You weren't selected by the school board, and we just can't believe it. What a team we would have made!

"But I was wondering," he added, "since you have such excellent experience in writing, could we call on you for some consulting?"

I relate these experiences to encourage you. Apparently, I made a favorable impression or this interview wouldn't have taken place. Now you can do that too. How are you looking these days? Is your grooming projecting what is necessary in order to compete? How does your voice sound—are you discouraged, sounding down in the mouth? Give yourself a little pep talk. Come on, you can do it. You are a Designer original. Project a positive self-image.

Don't try to make it just on your laurels, impressive and great as they may be. The competition is keen.

Analyze Obstacles

All age problems in job hunting are relative. For instance, being too young could mean that you're forty-five and shooting for a top spot in an industry where 90 percent of the top executives are ten years your senior. On the other hand, being too old could be a case of being thirty-two in the advertising field. My son, at the time of this writing, is in his early forties, and he has experienced some difficulty already in his occupational field. "The fresh-out-of-college guys with their degrees posted on the Internet, willing to work at half the salaries of seasoned guys like me, are edging us out," he told me. But he faced this challenge realistically, applied his own style of innovation, and maintained an upbeat attitude that landed him job interviews resulting in employment.

Those with "seasoned minds" need to analyze the obstacles to be overcome if goals are to be achieved. One of those obstacles relates to the terminology currently being used in the marketplace. This is especially true if you are seeking entrance into the corporate world. Become acquainted with the jargon of today's work world. Keep your vocabulary up-to-date to show potential employers that you are aware of what it takes to keep ahead in today's market.

Words are powerful. You will want to show creativity, curiosity, and intelligent forethought when being interviewed. Let your conversation create an impression that accurately reflects who and what you are, but avoid the temptation to be pretentious. Don't try to blow the interviewer away with how great you are. Poise and maturity are what the interviewer is looking for from mature people. You want to leave the interviewer thinking, *I think she would remain calm under fire. She showed good judgment* . . . (more on communication and interviewing skills in part 2).

I find it interesting in the literature I have researched that younger job seekers try to project maturity while older workers think they must project eternal youth. My advice for young job seekers is this: If you are young, maturity is key. You must project yourself as someone who is a down-to-earth and solid type of person—someone who can make good, sound judgments in a variety of situations.

Some interviewers will have preconceived ideas about older interviewees, and thus older job seekers may have to work harder to change interviewers' perceptions and prejudices. Today there appears to be a shift in favor of experience over youth. So don't underestimate your value.

Nonsense!

When someone told eighty-nine-year-old poet Dorothy Duncan that she had lived a full life, she responded tartly, "Don't you past tense me!"

A youth-oriented culture would try to say that a person's usefulness ends at sixty-five—if not sooner. But people like Dorothy Duncan recognize this for the nonsense it is and go right on leading productive lives.

- Artist Pablo Picasso was still producing paintings at ninety—and his painting became more innovative with the years.
- Pianist Arthur Rubinstein gave one of his greatest recitals at age eighty-nine.
- Actress Jessica Tandy won an Academy Award at eighty for her performance in *Driving Miss Daisy*.
- Congressman Claude Pepper of Florida was still actively championing the rights of the elderly and the poor at age eighty-eight.
- Environmentalist Marjory Stoneman Douglas, credited with saving the Everglades, was still fighting for the cause at age one hundred.
- After raising four sons, Lena Genser of Jersey City finished high school, obtained a college degree at age eighty-three, and took up computer programming at ninety.
- Real estate investor Eric de Reynier of Albany, California, took up hang gliding when he was seventy-two and was still at it in his eighties.
- Hulda Crooks of Loma Linda, California, climbed Mount Whitney for the twenty-third time at age eighty.

- Maggie Kuhn, forced to retire at sixty-five, founded the Gray Panthers to champion the rights of older people.
- At age eighty, President John Quincy Adams, when asked how he was, replied: "Mr. Adams is quite all right, thank you." His faith in God and his sense of humor helped, he maintained.
- Colonel Harlan Sanders was well into his sixties when he launched his Kentucky Fried Chicken empire.
- Conductor Leopold Stokowski renewed his recording contract for another five years when he was ninety-five.

Harvard University reported that of one hundred graduates who had retired at age sixty-five, seven out of eight were dead by age seventy-five. In a second group of a hundred who had worked beyond sixty-five, only one in eight had died by age seventy-five. Research suggests that retiring too early in life may significantly reduce one's longevity.

Most women now leave the workforce before they turn sixty; most men before they turn sixty-three. Not all are happy with this. According to a study in the *New York Times*, half of the elderly who are out of the workforce are satisfied with their situation, one-quarter are simply unable to work (presumably because of health), and one-quarter are very unhappy with the fact that they aren't working.

One man wrote that now at the age of seventy, he felt he was in every sense a younger, fresher man than he was at thirty: "At this present time I am in the strength of God, doing twice as much work, mental and physical, as I have ever done in the best days of the past, and this with less than half the effort necessary. My life, physical, mental, and spiritual, is like an artesian well—always full, overflowing."

In February 1901, Winston Churchill, slim and elegant at the age of twenty-six, rose to make his inaugural speech in the House of Commons. Here was the stage where, for the next fifty years, he would receive almost constant criticism and suffer many humiliating defeats. In those early years, according to one historian, Churchill "was probably the most hated man in the House of Commons." His enemies called him "The Blenheim Rat"—not exactly a term of respect.

Thirty-eight years later, when Great Britain was on the verge of collapsing from Hitler's attacks, King George VI asked Churchill to form a new government. By now Churchill was sixty-five, the oldest head of state in Europe. This crusty, elder statesman had lived a long time. He was too battle scarred to put on a false smile or to talk in Pollyannaish terms about the future. "I have nothing to offer but blood, toil, tears, and sweat," he told his countrymen that night in May 1940 with blunt realism. His fierce attitude conveyed the fact that he actually relished this coming combat. He believed the dispirited and ill-equipped British nation still controlled its own destiny.

And who can forget his memorable words after the fall of France: "We shall fight on the beaches. We shall fight on the landing grounds. We shall fight in the hills. We shall never surrender."

This mixture of realism and determined hope eventually won the day for the Allies in World War II. And it is this same mix that will give any of us the ability to achieve our own personal successes. It's been wisely said that if there were one huge tranquilizer that would make us oblivious to all of our problems, most of us wouldn't take it. That's because we know that trouble often brings out the best in us.

In speaking to a college group in San Jose, California, a few years ago, I mentioned that I'd been through many hills and valleys and that writing sometimes feels like I'm trying to walk up a hill with my ankles tied together. The students were interested and eager to learn from me, and I was only too happy to share with them. I asked for questions and comments. One young woman said, "Tell us more about the valleys," and I heard a chorus of "Yeahs" from all over the room. It was a moving experience. I ended by telling them what the psalmist said, and pointedly asked them if they were willing to accept the challenge he presented: "With the psalmist, could you say, 'You have relieved me in my distress'?" (Ps. 4:1).

Can you say that now?

Part 2

Where You Can Be Tomorrow

Knowing how to mount a hard-hitting job search is the key to becoming reemployed. Get ready to capitalize on your strengths and make the most of the talents, experience, and know-how you have.

Your tomorrow is what you make of it.

8

Turning the Corner

Without question, as you maneuver your way through the often murky channels of job hunting, you will encounter experiences that will throw you off balance. Some days it will be the accumulation of "thanks but no thanks" letters in your mailbox in response to your resumes, cover letters, and applications. At other times it may be the buildup of frustration that accompanies trying to learn something about a company to whom you are applying.

You will have days when nothing, absolutely nothing, you do seems to go right. I recall only too well one such day—I lost this book manuscript on the computer. I was devastated. That was one difficult day! Nevertheless, I remembered reading a conversation between Sir Winston Churchill and his wife that encouraged me.

When Churchill was turned out as prime minister after leading Great Britain through the darkest hours of its history, his wife tried to comfort him by telling him it was a "blessing in disguise." "If it is," said Churchill, "then it is very effectively disguised." But Mrs. Churchill had a point. After all, look what happened to Ronald Reagan after Warner Brothers released him. Or Lee Iacocca after Henry Ford fired him.[1]

I tried telling myself that everything that had happened, including the job loss, was a disguised blessing. But I had a hard time giving voice to the words. When I did, I felt like I would choke on what I was saying. At that point, I was thrust back on my faith.

I remembered the story of Tom Landry, former head coach of the Dallas Cowboys, who was replaced—"fired," in his words. He discovered that it was his faith, more than anything else, that enabled him to keep his perspective and not feel devastated or bitter about being fired. "And it's that faith," he said, "that gives me hope for whatever the future holds for me outside of professional football."

William Buckley, writing in *Reader's Digest*, points out that coming to terms with a crisis, whether it's the death of a loved one, divorce, illness, or loss of a job, is always painful. Yet some individuals move through such transitions gracefully. He asks, "What do these masters of change have going for them?"

Buckley answers his question by pointing to five things these people do. (1) They remember that optimism pays, (2) they take one step at a time, (3) they keep the faith, (4) they take stock, and (5) they take action.

Optimism Pays

There may come a point in your job search efforts when you stop, analyze, take stock, and say as I did, "Something's wrong. All this seems so fruitless, and costly too. I'm not doing something right."

At such times optimism pays. Buckley points to an optimistic attitude as a powerful motivator. I had sought to remain optimistic. I heeded the advice of such optimists as Earl Nightingale, who said, "When striving toward your goals, remember to hold the image of your success clearly before yourself at all times. Push beyond your perceived limitations, and keep failure out of your mind."

I adopted a "can do" approach, remembering Mary Crowley, president and founder of Home Interiors and Gifts, Inc., a Dallas-based direct-sales company. In an interview with her a few years before her death, she told me how she had walked the streets with CPAs, teachers, and bank presidents, looking for a job during the Great Depression. "I had very few marketable skills," she told me, adding, "but my grandmother had instilled in me that when things happen to you, you lose only if you react to them rather than using the experience to progress."

Mary chose to progress. With tenacity and a resilient attitude, she found the courage and determination to start over again. The result was her own business, which, at the time of my meeting with her, was a $400 million a year success, offering thousands of women across the country an opportunity to be self-employed.

I thought quite a bit about Mary Crowley in the days following my own job loss. I remembered her telling me that the day that had dawned with the funeral of her old career had ended with the birth of her own company. "Out of my disappointment came victory," she said, and I recalled how her eyes had brightened in memory. "This experience reinforced a lesson I had learned as a child. You never gain by sitting around feeling sorry for yourself. Attitude is the mind's paintbrush. It can color a situation gloomy and gray or cheerful and gay. In fact, attitudes are more important than facts."

I read about Sally Frame-Kasaks, chairman and CEO of the Talbots chain of specialty stores, who became a full buyer in retailing at age twenty-six. Her rise in retailing was spectacular: moving from president of Ann Taylor to Saks Fifth Avenue to Garfinckel's. Sidney Mayer, senior vice president for merchandise planning and coordination at Saks, explained how Sally beat out the other candidates for the vice president spot. Her knowledge and her dedication to quality were impeccable, but it was her personality that set her apart. "She had an effervescence that just didn't quit," he said.

"I owe my optimistic nature to a good Presbyterian up-bringing—a 'can do' approach to life," Sally maintained.[2]

I began to wonder if my optimism was slipping. Was I perhaps projecting something besides effervescent optimism? It was something to think about.

One Step at a Time

Buckley's second step to change is to take one step at a time. This step was no stranger to me. I have always lived on the assurance of Psalm 37:23–24, where we are reminded that the steps of a good man are ordered by the Lord; he sees us when we fall and picks us up. "The way of the LORD is strength for the upright. . . . The integrity of the upright will guide them" (Prov. 10:29; 11:3).

From the moment I lost my job, I wasted no time in updating my resume, watching newspaper and business journal ads, and composing personalized cover letters to accompany each resume sent out. I began researching at the library, making trips to city hall to scan job postings, and following through on tips and leads given to me. I networked by letting everyone I could think of know that I was seeking a position in keeping with my skills. I followed the advice of Richard Bolles in *What Color Is Your Parachute?* and others.

But what wasn't I doing that I should have been doing? That is a common question the unemployed ask. As you have seen in this book, unemployment can last a lot longer than we expect.

Keep the Faith

"Keep the faith," Buckley says. Indeed, I'd done that, bolstered by my husband's support as together we searched the Scriptures, read devotional books, and prayed.

Satan is our enemy, and he will use a variety of manipulations and means to hinder us. He is mean and deceptive. Sometimes God just "shuts us up to faith." The roster of biblical people who experienced this is long: Moses, Joseph, Paul and Silas, and the apostle John, to name just a few. If Joseph had never been Egypt's prisoner, he never would have become Egypt's governor. The chains about his feet ushered in the golden chain about his neck.

Right at the time when the manuscript was lost on the computer, I received a phone call.

"Helen, I've been thinking about your situation," the caller said. "I know your faith has been stretched incredibly in many ways in the past, and now it's being tested once again. For whatever it's worth, I honestly feel that because the two of you have demonstrated such faith, in many respects far more than many of us may ever experience, that God has taken you one step further in the walk of faith. Mere normal faith testing wouldn't do . . ."

I must confess that the experience of prolonged job loss was one of the severest tests of our faith that either my husband or I had ever faced. My husband's health was in decline, and I simply had to work. Once again I had to stop and think. *Faith. What is it really?* Many thoughts came to mind. The one that has been helpful to me may also prove to be of benefit to you. If you and I were to go down to the ocean's edge and watch a ship sail away until we couldn't see it any longer, would it mean that the ship was no longer real and not out there? Of course not! Just so, faith accepts what it cannot see. Faith believes beyond the optic nerve.

For some, this dimension of faith is a new approach to handling the crisis of job loss. But I can tell you that turning my fears over to God, sometimes many times during the course of even one day, empowered me as God infused me with hope and a vision for the future. I thought of the children of Israel. Joshua, their leader, gave them God's instructions. They were *not* to wait in their camps until the way was opened to the Promised Land. They were to move on, walking by faith. They were to break camp, pack up their goods, form a line to march, and move down to the very banks of the river before the Jordan would be parted.

Imagine it! There stretched the great Jordan River—at flood stage, no less—before them. How in the world were they going to get to the other side? If they had come down to the edge of the river and then stopped, waiting for the water to divide before they stepped into it, they would have waited in vain. They were told that as soon as the feet of the priests who bore the ark dipped into the water, the waters would heap up and they would be able to cross over on dry ground (Josh. 3:13).

Dare to step out in faith! God hasn't changed. He still honors faith that takes him at his word. The reason we are so often hindered is that we expect to see every difficulty removed before we try to pass through. When my husband and I uprooted and left behind our home and belongings and headed to the West Coast one fall day five months after my job loss, we felt as if we had put our feet into the water. Once we got there, we moved eight times in nine months. Yes, my faith had to go deeper.

Faith as a Lamp

Lloyd Douglas dramatizes faith magnificently in his classic book, *The Big Fisherman.* One scene in particular has always spoken to my heart.

"Don't forget," admonished Peter, "that we couldn't understand why he wanted to leave Canaan and come to Capernaum."

"That was different," mumbled Thomas. "We felt that he was urgently needed there."

"Maybe he feels that he is now needed elsewhere," observed Andrew, to which James added, "I don't believe he cares very much whether we understand him or not."

"You are right, Jimmy," rumbled old Bartholomew. "He's teaching us to have faith in him."

"But—can't a man have faith—and understanding too?" argued Thomas.

"No!" declared Bartholomew, bluntly. "That's what faith is for, my son! It's for when we can't understand."

"That's true!" approved Peter. "When a man understands, he doesn't need faith."

"I don't like to be kept in the dark," put in Philip.

"If a man has enough faith," replied Peter, "he can find his way in the dark—with faith as his lamp."[3]

That's the kind of faith we need as we confront our unemployment. Beyond where we can see, beyond what we are searching for, there is something that's real. What it requires from us is a steady, firm, fixed resolve to continue to do the near-at-hand things to bring order and stability into our lives, all the while believing that God is orchestrating the events that are taking place and is daily moving us nearer to what he has planned. Meanwhile, we trust, we pray, we claim biblical promises, we live a day at a time, a step at a time, in a moment-by-moment walk. Faith is to be our light. (Read Hebrews 11.)

Many Christian authors—including pastors, teachers, and psychiatrists—call faith the "most vital ingredient" of the resilience we need to cope with personal crisis.

Take Stock

Masters of change take stock, Buckley wrote. That's what I was doing as I paused in the midst of my daily job-search efforts. In doing this, I came to the realization that another course of action was required. My course of action will not necessarily be yours; what works for one person may not apply to someone else. What I learned, however, will most likely benefit you as you take stock of your situation.

A friend suggested that I meet a business friend of hers, a career counselor. I hesitated. I had already been to and investigated two executive recruitment agencies and had decided against them. (These were search firms where the agency is corporate-funded, that is, paid by the prospective employer. Other firms require the client to pay the fee, which can amount to a very hefty sum.)

Kenneth and Sheryl Dawson, in *Job Search: The Total System*, provide excellent advice that is worth heeding when it comes to search firms. They point out that job hunters who are emotionally vulnerable will pay upward of $5,000, $10,000, or $12,000 and get nothing but a resume and a list of target companies that hasn't been updated since their grandfather looked for a job. If someone wants your money for goods or services, that's fine—that's free enterprise. But if some low-life sponge tries to get your money in return for nothing but a lot of fast talk, fancy acronyms, and stacks of computer printouts, get out of there as quickly as you can. Then write to anyone and everyone you can think of—the Better Business Bureau, your representative in Congress, your mayor, your district attorney, your state legislator.

In other words, keep your money in your pocket. The vultures are out there ready to pounce on vulnerable job seekers. This is not a blanket indictment against all search agencies or career counselors. However, no one else can do all your work for you. Remember, rejection is part of the process in seeking to become employed, and anyone who promises he has a quick, surefire technique to get you a job is quite possibly a charlatan. Sometimes these people are referred to as "headhunters" or "recruiters." Typically they will demand a large up-front fee for their services. Beware!

Tom Sawyer, the career counselor my friend recommended, was not like that. He and other consultants like him provide career counseling on an hourly basis or through a complete career advancement program, and their fees are within reason. It is usually wise to have the recommendation of someone who knows or has used such a consultant.

Yellow Pages listings of career consultants include:

- Aptitude and Employment Testing
- Career and Vocational Counseling
- Executive Consultants
- Management Consultants
- Personnel Consultants
- Vocational Consultants

Richard Bolles cautions to choose career consultants very carefully. "You must do your own comparison shopping," he says, "and do your own sharp questioning before you ever sign up with anyone. If you don't, you will deserve whatever you get (or, more to the point, don't get)." *What Color Is Your Parachute?* provides a "sampler" of career counselors by state, but he emphasizes that it's just that, a sampler, for, if he were to list all the career counselors "out there," he would have to provide an encyclopedia! But you can find such help in your own area, and you may want to check his book to see if he has listed them. Otherwise, go to your local bookstore or library to get information.

What you receive in such a program depends, of course, on the counselor. Basically, what you should get is a market-based, value-building approach to career advancement. The initial meeting would require that you provide background information about yourself that includes your career history and professional goals. Where there is uncertainty about the direction those goals should take, and where a career change is being contemplated, a wise counselor will help you in assessing your strengths, skills, and weaknesses, and then advise and provide guidance on job-hunting techniques.

Perhaps you are thinking I could have done all that on my own. Yes, I probably could have, and I had done much on my own. And maybe you have too. I followed Bolles's advice and the suggestions of many others. But in my case, as may be true for you, I came to the place, probably exacerbated by the computer fiasco of losing this book manuscript, where I needed moral support and encouragement from someone like Tom.

In talking to others who have used such services, I discovered that most of us reach the point, especially after the job search becomes prolonged, at which we recognize and admit that if we are going to turn a corner, we need to invest in ourselves.

Take Action

"Take action" is Buckley's fifth bit of advice for change. I knew taking action in my case meant it was time to invest in myself. As with any other investment that costs money, I wanted to make sure it would yield a good return. You may need to ask yourself the question I asked of myself: "Am I a good investment?" When money is in short supply—as it is for most of us who find ourselves caught in a prolonged unemployment crunch—we have to be doubly cautious.

Again I would emphasize the need to be discerning when choosing a professional agency. I never would have agreed to work with a career counselor who demanded full payment up front. Neither would I have agreed to sign a contract stipulating payments. Anything that appeared gimmicky would have sent up red flags in my head. Beyond research, comparison shopping, and sharp questioning, trust your intuitive senses.

Investing in yourself can take different forms. Professional assistance will help you better understand your potential. Once your strengths, liabilities, and personal goals are understood, a career counselor will help you identify career and industry directions you may never even have considered. He will also help develop a marketing plan, structuring a complete personal action program just for you, and write superior resumes and cover letters about you. Moreover, he will show you how to research the job market locally and geographically in those parts of the country where you are willing to go and where your particular skills are in demand. You will also be taught interviewing skills and be given administrative and marketing support.

Sometimes people ask me if going to a career counselor showed a lack of faith. Wasn't the strength I am so big on asking God to provide forthcoming? Of course it was there, and I was drawing on it. In no way am I implying that God was not sufficient to meet my needs. But sometimes we need someone with skin on his nose to help see us through our crisis moments. This too I came to regard as God's provision.

As is the habit of my heart, I sought God's leading in my choice of career counselor. This is an advantage we who are God's children have, but I have discovered that so few realize this when they are caught in the dilemma of job loss.

When I experience inner peace, I know God is providing assurance that I'm on the right track.

Do not let your zeal slacken, be fervent, continue to serve and trust the Lord, rejoice in hope, be patient in tribulation, continue steadfastly in prayer.

Romans 12:11–12, author's paraphrase

9

The Market-Driven Approach

When you go to buy a new appliance, a piece of furniture, a car, or a house, does the salesperson point out to you all the good features of what you are thinking of purchasing? Of course! Just so, in the market-driven approach to finding a job that matches the passions of your heart, you have to identify marketable assets. How else is the prospective employer to know?

Probably one of the most important things the career consultant did was to help me see myself in the right perspective. Think about this: From childhood on we are taught not to think too highly of ourselves (see Rom. 12:3; 1 Cor. 4:6–7). There's nothing wrong with such admonitions. What is wrong is our interpretation of them as we downplay what we have rightfully accomplished through the wise use of the gifts God has entrusted to us.

Harvey Mackay says in *Swim with the Sharks*, "What's the matter with being proud of what we have done or think we can do? In my opinion, humility is what our parents and teachers try to stuff us with when we're six years old to make us easier to handle, but it's unnatural."[1] He says the next time someone insinuates that you are egotistical, don't forget to thank them: "They have just provided a strong endorsement of your mental health. 'Self-esteem' is a buzzword these days, and it's about time. The higher it is, the better you get along with yourself, with others, and the more you'll accomplish."

I understand the need to tread cautiously when discussing a subject such as this. Certainly arrogance and boastfulness are distasteful. However, people who have lost their jobs tend to denigrate themselves. When we put ourselves down and fail to call attention to our genuine accomplishments, denying the importance and validity of something we have done, we short-circuit the job-search process.

A Career Checkup

As Tom and I sat together working on the material that would go into a new resume, he asked questions relating to my past, and I responded with ease. I felt comfortable sharing my work history and life accomplishments. His opinion was independent, unbiased, objective. I noticed he was taking notes. I felt like a patient in a doctor's office. Indeed, I was having a "career checkup."

Later, as we pulled out statements and words to use and he began mapping out the resume, I found myself protesting: "But Tom, that's bragging. I can't say that about myself on paper . . ."

And right there was one of the major clues as to what had been wrong with my job search. Tom looked at me with surprise. I looked back at him. Then we both started laughing. It was really so absurd.

Mackay points out that humility is an overrated emotion. Many of us were taught when we were young that the two worst human failings are lying and bragging. He says, "I'd rather stick with Will Rogers, who said, 'If you done it, it ain't bragging.'" I honestly had to learn to say that!

Mackay calls the right attitude plain old optimism. Others might label it PMA—a positive mental attitude. Regardless of its name, the right attitude is a practical success tool we can use to dramatically improve the results we get in our careers and in our lives. Brian Tracy, a recognized leader in the field of human development, points out that every serious researcher he has studied eventually has come to the conclusion that a positive mental attitude is the key to opening the door to one's future.

Mackay asks, "How can you be any good unless you think you can accomplish what you are not supposed to be able to accomplish?" He calls optimism a quality that consistently delivers results. And that's what you and I need when we are confronted with the harsh realities of pursuing a job. Does your resume reflect all that is marketable about you? Based on your resume and your cover letter and what you will say when you are interviewed, if you were a piece of merchandise, would you buy you?

Tom immediately identified one of the hindering factors that was keeping me from projecting myself into words on paper. I needed a good mind overhaul to revise the way I thought about myself. Howard Figler, in *The Complete Job-Search Handbook*, says modesty is truly the curse that kills a thousand careers; it's the back door of one's existence, a hedge. "Go on, admit it," says Figler. "You've done certain things well before, and you'll do them again."[2]

Career consultants help us see ourselves in the best possible light by looking not only at what we have accomplished, but also at our future potential as well. This is a part of the value-building communications strategies they employ. For instance, look at some of the skills found in a cross section of careers, and circle those that apply to you. I think you will look at yourself a lot differently when you are finished.

administer programs well
advise people
analyze data
appraise services
arrange functions
assemble apparatus
audit financial records
budget expenses
calculate data
classify records
coach others
collect money
communications expertise
confrontation skills
counseling expertise
creative and innovative
delegation skills
design capabilities
distribution of products
dramatizing ideas or problems
editing publications
entertaining people
evaluating situations and people
events coordinator abilities
expressing feelings
finding information
good listener
handling complaints
have a lot of endurance
inspecting objects
interpreting language
interviewing people
inventing new ideas
investigating problems
lobbying
locating missing information
managing
measuring boundaries

mediating
meeting the public
monitoring others
negotiation
operating equipment
organizing people and tasks
persuading others
planning agendas
politicking
preparing materials
printing
programming computers
promoting events
protecting property
reading volumes of material
recording scientific data
recruiting people
rehabilitating people
remembering data
repairing most anything
researching
running meetings
selling
serving
setting up demonstrations
sketching
speaking in public
supervising others calmly
take criticism well
teaching
tolerating interruptions
updating information and files
value integrity
visualizing new formats
work well with hands
working with precision
writing

Some career counselors administer psychological tests designed to measure interests and abilities. The two most commonly used tests are the Myers-Briggs Type Indicators and the Strong-Campbell Interest Inventory. These are multiple-choice tests designed to help you understand your personality, interests, and possible career paths that would work for you.

Some personality and interest tests can be taken on the Internet. Bolles recommends the Personality Questionnaire related to the Myers-Briggs test. Another is the Keirsey Character Sorter, related to the Myers-Briggs test. I strongly recommend Richard Bolles's latest book itself; you just can't go wrong listening to him.

Unfortunately, some people go to career counselors only to take aptitude and personality tests, wrongly expecting to find some sort of easy "scientific" answer to a career or job dilemma. Of course, this is a mistaken assumption, as many writers and career counselors point out.

It is very important to have a competent career counselor who knows how to interpret test results abstractly and is able to help you in your job decisions by taking into account what he or she has learned about your particular situation. Locating such a counselor will require careful research on your part.

The Creative Approach to Selling Yourself

Howard Figler points out self-marketing as the ultimate transition skill to carry you from one job to the next, because it allows you to see links between what you are doing now and the work you will choose tomorrow.

Selling yourself is a three-step process:

1. Give potential employers some reasons to want you (distinguish yourself from the competition).

2. Tell them stories about yourself. Stories explain without having to explain. In other words, they show you as a problem solver, revealing what you have done and leading the listener to believe that you can do it again.
3. Develop your social skills (selling your personality).[3]

Figler adds:

> Self-marketing is important because you must make the fullest possible use of your past experience when seeking a change of work; otherwise you are judged on the basis of superficial credentials and other external criteria, such as test scores, manner of dress, and prestige of previous employers. Your ability to communicate your worth is a function of your ability to recognize value in your own experience and see how it can be translated into new capabilities.[4]

There is probably much more to you than meets the eye. You may not even be aware of what is important in marketing yourself. Some career consultants have a strategy they use to help uncover your marketability potential as they seek to identify your career history. By taking some time to think about who you are and what you have done, you will get a picture of your potential. Therefore, get out a pad of paper and review every aspect of your life.

Here are things to cover: personal data; education; travel (states and countries in which you have resided) and willingness to relocate (where in the United States and/or overseas); languages (speak, read, write); military service (summary of assignments, status, honors, special schools and training); leisure activities (sports—skiing, tennis, etc.) and/or other interests (painting, gardening); nonemployment achievements (awards, professional societies, business memberships, offices held, committees or boards served on, copyrights, patents, inventions, articles or books published); reading (indicate your preferences in magazines, trade periodicals, business journals, books); references (personal, business, academic, social).

If you will put some work into it, this framework will give you more than just a snapshot of where you have come from in your career. You will have a kind of motion picture for each of your employment experiences. Start thinking in terms of the situations you have been in and the duties and opportunities that presented themselves. Now think of the actions you took and the results you achieved. This story-telling format is designed to help you uncover information about yourself that is both factual and persuasive. It really works.

Divide a sheet of paper across the top into columns to represent as many positions you have held that you feel you wish to analyze and highlight later on in your resume. (You may need to turn the paper sideways to allow more room for columns.) Then down the side of the paper, section off spaces for the name of the company, division, location, and dates you were there. In the next section, indicate the type of business and a description of the products and relevant information. In the next block, write the titles you held with dates (most recent first) and to whom you reported (titles, not names). In the next section, put your starting and ending salary and bonuses. And in the last box, write the reason for leaving (termination, left for more money, unfriendly takeover, reorganization of company, little room for advancement, unchallenged, etc.).

On additional pages describe each of these positions in more detail. Aim to provide a description of the general nature of the job. Here are suggestions:

Accounting	Business Development
Administration	Communications and/or Public Relations
Administrative Support	Credit
Agribusiness Consulting	Distribution
Assurance and/or Safety	Engineering

Environmental Services
Facilities Construction
Finance
General Management
Hospital Administration
Hourly Paid Worker
Human Resources/Personnel
Investor Relations
Legal
Marketing
Operations, Materials, or Facilities
   Management

Petroleum Consulting
Process Consulting
Production or Project Management
Purchasing
Quality Control
Sales
Secretarial Support
Senior Management
Systems

Amplify in separate paragraphs the purpose of the job, its scope of influence, number of people you may have supervised and their titles, budget, equipment and material responsibilities, the functional areas of authority and responsibility (e.g., market planning, research, sales, advertising promotions), other departments with whom you had liaison, and your range of contacts both inside and outside the organization. This exercise should give you a good grasp of how you are going to be able to market yourself in terms of situations, opportunities, and duties.

The final aspect of this exercise is to describe actions taken by you or others and the results achieved. Every source I consulted, including the career counselor, stressed the importance of using action verbs. Using another sheet of paper, think of descriptive key phrases, words, and concepts to describe your achievements and strengths in each position. The time you invest in doing this will have significant value when it comes to writing your resume and cover letter and/or working with a professional resume writer.

The word that starts the phrase must be a strong, active-voice verb. Here are some suggestions:

accepted	administered	advised
achieved	adopted	aided

analyzed
apprised
approved
arranged
assembled
assessed
assumed
attended
built
calculated
carried out
catalogued
checked
clarified
classified
collected
compiled
computed
conceived
conducted
conferred
constructed
consulted
contributed
controlled
cooperated
coordinated
correlated
counseled
created
decided
delegated
delivered
demonstrated
described
designed
determined
developed
devised

directed
discovered
distributed
doubled
earned
engineered
enlarged
established
estimated
evaluated
examined
exchanged
expanded
expedited
experienced
experimented
explained
facilitated
familiarized
formulated
furnished
gathered
generated
guided
halted
handled
headed
helped
implemented
improved
indexed
informed
innovated
inspected
inspired
installed
instituted
instructed
integrated

interpreted
interviewed
invented
investigated
justified
laid out
led
made
maintained
managed
mediated
negotiated
observed
operated
ordered
organized
originated
overcame
participated
performed
planned
procured
produced
projected
promoted
proved
provided
received
recommended
rectified
reduced
reorganized
represented
researched
reshaped
reviewed
revised
rewrote
scheduled

searched	strengthened	transformed
sent	studied	transmitted
service	submitted	tripled
simplified	suggested	unified
sold	supervised	used
solved	systemized	utilized
sorted	tailored	verified
specified	trained	wrote
straightened	transacted	

A careful use of these descriptive key words will capture the reader's attention, encouraging the eye to move along to read other critically important words that are illustrative of your potential worth. (In particular you will be using these key words and phrases in your cover letter and also in the interview itself.) Avoid passive descriptions and use of the word *I* (e.g., "Established and implemented communications policies and guidelines that successfully reshaped the image of the organization"). Results are most impressive when you can attach a dollar or percentage figure (e.g., "Created collateral material and directed all publicity and media events for a program that produced $5 million in revenue").

Phrases like these make you come across as an achiever, a person who is a doer. Subtly, but succinctly, you are underscoring your abilities and skills. Be certain, however, that your phrases can be backed up with facts or figures. Don't make inflated claims that have no substance in actual accomplishments.

Researchers point out that this kind of thinking utilizes the left (analytical) side of our brains to fully record all the factual aspects of our background and utilizes the right (creative) side in viewing ourselves in the most innovative fashion possible. For sure it's work, and it requires time and effort, but it does reap results. Your resume, cover letter, and you personally, when an interview develops, will come across as refreshing and interesting. You will be seen as someone the interviewer will seriously want to consider hiring.

To help you get started, here are a few additional brief grab 'em kind of statements:

- Developed programs that were delivered on time within budget and met all marketing objectives.
- Identified a $17 million market and created and managed a professional sales group to go after it.
- Devised a new concept in a tooling procedure that reduced costs by $200,000.

You may discover that writing these statements can actually be fun. You will surprise yourself at how valuable you are and what terrific accomplishments are yours. Go ahead—pat yourself on the back and talk about them. Remember Will Rogers: "If you done it, it ain't bragging." This is going to make you shine like a star. You deserve it.

My career counselor called these statements bullets: "Your aim with them is to hit the target. You're going for the bull's-eye!" We used round black symbols in front of each statement and indented them from the body of the cover letter so they stood out. (We'll talk more about the cover letter in chapter 11.)

Mind Mapping

Another exercise the career consultant took me through involved a fun process called "mind mapping." It is widely used in management circles and was originally developed in the early 1970s by British author and brain researcher Tony Buzan. It was further developed and applied in numerous creative ways by Michael Gelb, whose book *Present Yourself* is recommended by Judith Dubin and Melanie Keveles as being one of the best on the subject.

Here's how mind mapping works. Tom took a large piece of unlined paper and drew a stick figure in the center. "That's you," he said.

"Thanks a lot," I responded. "I should be that thin!"

You might put yourself in the center with a happy face, a cheerful reminder that will smile back at you each time you look at it.

"Now let's focus on your areas of expertise," Tom said. We used symbols or a word or combination of words to represent these areas: a book for books authored, $$$ for fund-raising efforts, etc. With a large colored marker, the mind map began to take shape, and I visually saw my skills and abilities portrayed with many lines radiating from the central figure.

"Now I want you to think of words representing various positions that would be a good fit for your talents," he said.

Since I am an acquisitions editor, editorial consultant, and writer/editor, those words surfaced, as well as marketing communications, public relations, advertising, and research. Your list of action verbs will be helpful in getting your mind going.

Let's say you are a product designer. Your mind map would no doubt show a variety of creative concepts, such as control consoles for stage, TV, and motion picture lighting equipment. It might show computer peripherals, desktop modems, bezel detailing, pocket pagers, respirator cabinet design, laser plotter interface controller, and so on. The brain loves pictures and images and remembers them more easily than words, so wherever possible, use little drawings.

Whatever your profession and your unique combination of skills, mind mapping is a technique that just might open up your mind to long-submerged options, fields, or other career possibilities you have overlooked and in which you might be happier and even more productive.

Tom encouraged me to think out loud as we interacted about employment possibilities that could be offshoots of each symbol or word. As you look over your mind map, you will see patterns emerging, a sort of blueprint as it were, of where you have been with your life, and you will have a visual plan to help in constructing your resume.

Assessing Your Strengths and Weaknesses

In talking to human resource managers, I learned that many final hiring decisions are based on what those doing the interviewing perceive to be an individual's personal strengths. Having a clear understanding of the strengths you have to offer and learning how to communicate this to others is very important. How would those who have worked with you describe you?

Interviewers are human. We might regard them with trepidation, but they are subject to the same foibles as you and me. Therefore, they are going to remember specifics more than vague generalities. This being true, provide them with something that will be memorable and stay with them after the interview (e.g., "One of my greatest strengths relates to my interpersonal skills . . ."). Expand on the statement.

When asked to mention a weakness, turn it into a strength, something that makes you sound even more employable (e.g., "When I get started on a project, I don't like interruptions. My husband says I hardly come up for air.").

Kathryn and Ross Petras point out that admitting to true weaknesses may harm you. A prospective employer might admire your honesty but wouldn't hire you. Two major mistakes are common and should be avoided at all costs: (1) the gut-honest answer, admitting to your major weaknesses, and (2) giving a canned response that sounds rehearsed. Just give examples that *sell you*.

Certainly don't mention any faults such as nervousness, sloppiness, carelessness, or anything that might impinge in any way on the position for which you are being considered. To nudge your thinking, here are some words that others might use to describe you.

achiever	diplomatic	kind
adaptable	discerning	loyal
alert	efficient	methodical
analytical	eloquent	observant
attentive	energetic	orderly
broad-minded	enthusiastic	organized
caring	fair	patient
composed	flexible	pleasant
conceptual	friendly	poised
considerate	genuine	reliable
consistent	good-natured	sincere
courteous	honest	tactful
creative	imaginative	tolerant
decisive	innovative	wise
dependable	intuitive	

Transferable Skills

A term used frequently by job searchers is *transferable skills*—probably the single most important concept in viewing how personal skills are usable in career development. Begin incorporating it in your repertoire of usable phrases. In my case, I was told that the ability to write effectively and in clear, readable language is valued highly in private industry, government agencies, educational institutions, and nonprofit organizations. Most of the skills that are important in any responsible job are applicable in a wide variety of work contexts. In other words, they are *transferable*.

As you take the time to come up with words and phrases that reflect who you are, what you do best, and where you are coming from, you should begin to see yourself as some-

142

one of value with a stockpile of marketable assets. Figler suggests five ways to identify skills and tap into your particular strengths:

1. from personal achievements
2. from a happy role you have occupied
3. from a peak experience
4. from a skills inventory and assessment (such as the one provided in this chapter)
5. from the feedback of family, friends, and acquaintances (even former co-workers) who may see attributes that you have overlooked yourself[5]

He points out that even what appear to be "shady but nonetheless marketable" things about you can be used to your advantage. He says that even former criminals can become outstanding law enforcers. Consider someone who is good at getting out of doing things or is a champ at nagging people to get things done. Now think about how those things could be turned into positives in seeking a job.

A friend of mine is a published composer, a concert pianist, a truly gifted person. As is true with so many artists, her work is usually a case of feast or famine. At one point she wasn't finding work in keeping with what she wanted to do. I challenged her to look for work at the big, glitzy department store in the mall near where she lived. "I love going in there just to hear the concert pianist," I said, adding, "I'll bet they are always looking for people like you." And they were!

The point: don't just depend on the one outstanding talent or venue that may have served you well for years.

Vocational Rigor Mortis

According to Figler, the biggest basket cases in getting on with their careers are professional athletes, college professors denied tenure, beautiful women whose physical charms have faded, artists who haven't found an immediate market, and others who have depended on a single talent for many years.

> Their problem can be stated simply: It is not necessary for them to build other skills as long as the one big talent is working for them, drawing acclaim and winning temporary rewards, so by the time the one big talent fades, a vocational rigor mortis, known as learned helplessness, has set in. The talented one has been fussed over, catered to, and provided for. The whole idea of struggling along like us working stiffs has been anathema.[6]

Vocational rigor mortis encompasses a lot more unemployed people than is recognized. Decline after a period in the limelight is a very real problem. There are "hidden charms in multipotentiality," and without question, most people possess a cluster of abilities that have long gone unrecognized.

You may be someone who has the option of choosing future activities that will nurture skills in keeping with what you already do well and have practiced in a nonpaid lifetime of experience. Volunteer work brings out latent abilities in many people. If you are a homemaker, for instance, who has served in volunteer capacities, or a recently divorced woman seeking to reenter the job market, don't underestimate your potential.

Don't worry about all the skills someone else may have that you don't feel you have. Forget about trying to measure up to someone else. Concentrate on who you are—your creativity, decision-making abilities, intuitiveness, thoroughness, logical thinking, ability to get along with people, and so on. Probably the most common mistake people make in job hunting is to disqualify themselves before the horse race even starts.

Don't let others define for you what they think you can or cannot do. Their information can be helpful, true, but it may also contain bias. Take care not to make someone else's opinions your own. Don't fail to take into account that likeability, motivation, leadership skills, ambition, and many other factors count right alongside experience.

When You're Sick and Tired of Looking for Work

At times you are going to feel "overdosed on the job search." As one person said, "I'm tired and beat and feeling like a jerk. I am weary of putting myself on the line, being evaluated, scrutinized, chewed up, and spit out. The energy and enthusiasm that you recommend is nice in theory, but it just feels like a poor acting job now. I've ruled out drugs or a facelift. Got any brilliant ideas about how to revive me?"[7]

Figler offers some of the best advice I've found for those stuck on the job-search merry-go-round in his book *The Complete Job-Search Handbook*, which I've referred to in preceding chapters. The following list includes a combination of things he suggests and things I did to breathe fresh air into the job search.

1. Consider seeking the assistance of a professional counselor.
2. Check with your local unemployment office, professional organizations, and civic organizations, or watch the paper for meetings you could attend where job-search support groups meet. On the recommendation of my job counselor, I joined a professional group. I started receiving their literature, which in itself opened my eyes to additional opportunities and happenings in my field.
3. Continue networking. Even though you have contacted everyone you could think of before, if it has been

any length of time at all, reconnect, reminding them of your need for employment. My own reemployment finally came as a result of someone for whom I had worked twenty years earlier remembering me. He knew that when we had talked seventeen months earlier, I had just lost my job. We reconnected, and the result was a position for myself, as well as one for my husband. (Swallow your pride. I know networking can get wearisome both for you and your contacts, but take a close look at how you have been networking. Are you doing or saying anything that is turning people off?)

4. Back off from networking. I'm not contradicting myself; I'm simply pointing out that some people assume networking is the end product in the job search, and it isn't always. If you have worn out your welcome with people you know, back off. Don't put all your eggs in one basket and rely too heavily on "help" from others.

5. Broaden your range of potential employers. Have you been focusing too narrowly? Expand your thinking. Spread your wings.

6. Really hurting financially? Unemployment benefits exhausted? Consider part-time or temporary work more seriously, or take a job in an entirely unrelated arena. You need money coming in? Do what you have to do. Use an interim job as a bridge to get from where you are now to where you want to be.

7. Get involved with some community and social groups. You will connect with people that way. You may not feel up to socializing and putting your best foot and face forward, but give it a try. You might be pleasantly surprised at what happens. Develop some new relationships.

8. Let everyone you meet know that you are looking for a job—the mailman, the hairstylist, people at places

where you shop, church members, neighbors. Even go so far as to give them a copy of your resume. It can't hurt.

9. Consider going back to school for training in another field, upgrading your field, or retraining if necessary. "Retooling by schooling" is often oversold as a method of career advancement, but in today's job climate, it may be a necessity for some. I looked into real estate, interior design, and the paralegal field, and I would have gone into one of those fields if I hadn't received a job offer. These were fields of interest to me. Now may be your opportunity to move into another line of work that is of interest to you.

10. Check out nonprofit organizations and offer your work experience in exchange for learning something about the nonprofit sector. Don't forget volunteerism. Figler points out that working for a person who can teach you about a field used to be called apprenticeship, and it has a rich history.

11. Figler says, "Fatigue is the backwash of rejection. You're bound to lose energy after a certain number of nos." So what can you do?

a. Back off completely from the job search. Incubate. Give your mind a chance to rest: "Incubation activities rejuvenate the spirit, and your mind can ease into reflection without your forcing it to THINK." Figler is right. Pick up shells on the beach or watch a bird, squirrels, your grandkids, or your own children at play. Do something totally different.

b. Break the cycle. You may be beating a dead horse. We broke the cycle by going to the West Coast. Then we broke the cycle again by returning to the Midwest when our home hadn't sold and I hadn't located a position. Don't fear change.

c. Get off the production line. "Overdosing can come

from an excess of job-search activity, from sheer quantities of time spent. . . ." Figler calls it too much quantity and not enough quality. Get with friends. Play a tabletop game. Have a stimulating conversation with someone you really enjoy being around.

d. Dig out of your ruts. Read a good book. Catch up on your magazine reading. Write some letters. Call your friends and say, "Hey, I need a change of pace. What do you suggest?"

12. Now get excited again and start tooting your own horn. You may need to rewrite your resume. Admittedly, the time spent identifying and choosing the right ingredients for your resume may seem an eternity. But before you stop short, remember that these foundational efforts are going to allow you to transform boring, prosaic truth into interesting, marketable truth.

13. Keep on knocking and asking God to intervene on your behalf. At one point when I was exhausted and discouraged, a call from an editor friend helped to turn the tide. "Helen, you've just got to keep on knocking and asking God to open doors for you," Mary Ruth said. "You can't give up." Her reference was to the biblical injunction, "For everyone who keeps on asking receives, and he who keeps on seeking finds, and to him who keeps on knocking it will be opened" (Matt. 7:8 AMP; see also Luke 11:10).

I did what the Bible said, and it wasn't easy. (I won't deceive you.) But I believe that in God's perfect time, he opened the door for us, and when we walked through, we knew it was right. He will do that for you too.

Our Lord prayed at every crisis in his life. Surely we are not misled if we follow in his steps. We are praying to a father—to our heavenly Father. As his children, we can approach him with confidence. And whether he gives, withholds, or delays, it is always an expression of infinite mercy and Fatherly love. He knows the end from the beginning. He is never early; but neither is he ever late.

10

Resumania

A lot of resumes look about as thrilling as an obituary! They are dead and boring, and there isn't a shred of evidence that the person is an alive, exciting, enthusiastic, committed human being.

Advice regarding resume writing is so diverse it will make your head swim. One person will say that the passionate belief in resumes is out of proportion with how often they get anyone an interview for a job. Someone else feels that it is a mistake to use your resume as a leading player in your job search and that it shouldn't be the centerpiece of your presentation.

Robert Half, author of *How to Get a Better Job in This Crazy World*, says, "Writing a resume need not be an exercise in pursuit of the Nobel Prize in literature. In fact, quite the opposite is true. A resume ideally states, clearly and accurately, what you have accomplished in your work life. It should also indicate to a prospective employer what you can bring to the company."[1]

Others claim the resume is the strongest marketing tool you can use. It's your PR agent, your personal advertisement, your calling card, the key method of self-promotion. They believe the importance of a well-written resume cannot be overstated.

There's truth in what all of these people are saying. A diversified strategy (packaging and marketing yourself in different ways beyond just sending out resumes) is essential, but I have yet to meet anyone who was able to make direct contact with a hiring authority without a resume. Even those who networked successfully still needed a resume.

Frankly, I don't see how you can get by without getting your credentials and job experiences down on paper. And I believe almost everyone needs objective help in designing and writing a resume (even the most experienced writers can be mystified as to how best to present themselves). So honor your resume, as it sets the tone and direction for all that you do in your job search.

You will find some experts saying you don't need someone writing your resume, and you shouldn't go to a resume-preparation service or copy the formats you see in books. These experts point out that the desks of hiring executives are piled high with resumes that have the same format, take the same approach, and often use the same words.

Certainly you don't want your resume to look like it's canned. You want it to be attention getting. Whether you write it yourself or have it done, it is up to you to provide the material that will achieve the desired effect. You will find books on resume writing and the work of enterprising resume writers helpful in your task. You can also find help on the Internet. Writing a resume to be used via the Internet calls for some creative approaches that differ in some respects from the traditional paper resume.

Electronic Resumes

If you don't want your resume to get overlooked, and that possibility certainly exists according to everything I've read regarding electronic resumes, then key words should be used. These differ, of course, depending on the company, the type of position for which you are applying, and the person in charge of choosing the key words. Here are some examples: *word processing, data entry, technical writing, customer service, problem solving, financial analysis, administrative, database use, telephone, desktop publishing, accounting, spreadsheet use.* Your creativity will show when you carefully study the posted ad for a position and note the terminology used by the company to whom you are applying. Respond to the ad using the terms used in the ad.

There is no basic agreement on the number of Internet sites devoted to job hunting; it ranges from a thousand to one hundred thousand or more! The purpose of Internet sites is to make it easier for the job hunter and the prospective employer to find each other. With a hundred million American adults having access to the Internet (a figure that will be outdated even before this book gets published), the chances of your resume getting a decision maker's attention seems slim. Still, it happens, and it's estimated that 58 million Americans are online every day. How many of those people are looking for a job? But you could be one of the fortunate ones. So it's a gamble, a crapshoot someone might say!

Where do you post your resume? Ideally, where employers have sites listing their jobs. Richard Bolles recommends some of the more prominent job sites that have what he calls a "search while you sleep" capability. These include www.monster.com, www.hotjobs.com, www.flipdog.com, www.headhunter.net, www.careerbuilder.com, www.salary.com, www.jobs.com, www.joboptions.com, and www.eurojobs.com. He says, quoting someone else, that trying to catalog the Internet is like trying to catalog a mudslide. Some of the sites alive and flourishing one day may disappear the next![2]

I'm not intending to discourage you, but Bolles cites two studies that illuminate how small a number of jobs are found through the Internet. One study of three thousand Internet-using job seekers showed that only 4 percent actually landed a job by going online. Another discovered that only 8 percent of employers' new hires were derived from the Internet. Bolles's book and others will inform you of the pitfalls and successes of online job hunters' experiences. Joyce Lain Kennedy says that online job hunting isn't likely to produce results.[3]

Even as I was completing the writing of this material, I made a trip to the post office and, as usual, had to stand in line. I use this standing-in-line time to get acquainted with people, and in front of me was a young father with his fourteen-month-old son. "So what do you do for a living?" I asked.

"You won't believe it," he warmly responded. "I was without work for ten days, and I got a job through the Internet."

"You're kidding!" I said, shocked to my sandals (remembering what I'd just written)!

"Just out of the blue, no advance warning, a bunch of us were let go where I worked. We've only lived here four years; moved here, in fact, for the job. So what did I do? I got on the Internet, and it worked for me. Yeah, we're moving back to where we came from, and I give all the credit to www .careerbuilder.com." He was one excited young daddy!

With more than 16 million resumes at any given time floating around the Internet, in what another author calls "data smog," how can you best use the Internet? Bolles gives five ways the Internet can help with job hunting: (1) testing and counseling; (2) research—of fields, jobs, organizations, and salaries; (3) networking; (4) job postings; and (5) resume posting.

Potentially Winning Resumes

I attended a library-sponsored workshop for the unemployed in Silicon Valley, California. The purpose was to educate attendees about library research and how it could benefit the unemployed. Forty-two people attended—fourteen men, the rest women. When it came time to introduce us to resume writing, the presenter said, "We have more than forty books available for you to use." Your library will also have such resources available.

If you use the services of a professional resume writer, you will get the most for your money if you go in having done your homework (what we talked about in the last chapter). After looking at your material and talking with you, a professional should advise which is the best format for you to use in keeping with your skills and background and provide samples. A career counselor will suggest the actual layout and construct the resume with your help.

The president of a manufacturing company in Indiana wrote an article titled "A Little Advice from an Interviewer." He said that employers recognize that resumes, letters, and interviews are part of a game, a scripted routine, so a professionally prepared resume is okay provided it doesn't look like a glitzy press release. Pastel, quasi-designer paper with fancy typefaces didn't score marks with him, nor would it with most decision makers. (Rare exceptions would be for someone in graphic arts or some other creative field.) He received some resumes headlined "Ability, Integrity, Education." "Come on, folks," this corporate president said, "the name of the game is to impress the prospective employer with proven accomplishments, not show-biz formats. These we discarded."

Remember, the person who reads your resume isn't an idiot. What renders a resume useless is what is in it. Yours won't get lost in the shuffle if you commit yourself to writing the best resume possible. And if you need help, get it.

For a professional appearance, use black type on 8 ½ by 11 inch white or off-white cotton-fiber bond paper (25 percent rag content), preferably with a quality "feel." Don't include photographs or drawings, and never mention your pay level. You do not have to say why you left a particular job. If it comes up, you can disclose that during the interview. (Be prepared for such a question by having some kind of statement in mind as to why you left a job.) *Never* include personal information in a resume—height, weight, marital status. Who cares! None of that has any bearing whatsoever on your ability to do a job.

It is not necessary to type "Resume" at the top. That's a trivial redundancy. Don't clutter the page with nonessentials or extraneous words that steal time from the twenty seconds (or less) you have to grab the scanner's attention. White space is important, so don't crowd information. Let your resume breathe.

Opinions vary on the length a resume should be. If you have reason to make your resume longer than the usual prerequisite pages (two), go for it. If your experience is such that it requires more space, I see no reason to shorten it just to conform. Don't, however, bloat your resume with un-needed information. Use discretion. Be wise. Send the resume unfolded with a white cardboard (to keep it from getting bent in transit) in a large white envelope. And remember, every resume should be accompanied by a well-crafted letter. (More on the cover letter in chapter 11.)

Since resume preparation is covered in detail in many books and on the Internet, I have chosen not to include samples. What I do provide are tips on writing resumes gleaned from many sources and an assessment of what works best. Some of these tips and facts may surprise, disturb, or even alarm you as they did me, but I think you will find that they help keep the job search in perspective.

The Stuff Resumes Are Made Of

Possibly the most important thing to remember when writing your resume is that telling prospective employers the facts is never enough. You have to market yourself as a product. In fact, that is the secret to writing a high-voltage resume. Position yourself in such a way that you come off as a highly desirable marketable commodity.

Those doing the screening of resumes tell us that only two to five out of every hundred normally survive; 95 to 98 percent don't make the cut. But yours can. You can have the competitive edge.

The vice president of a personnel agency told me that many applicants make the mistake of assuming that putting down descriptions of responsibilities for their previous jobs is enough. He emphasized, "In this extremely competitive market, employers are looking more for what an individual can bring to a company in the way of initiative, innovativeness, and leadership. To catch the eye of an employer, resumes should clearly state how the applicant helped previous employers save money, improve visibility, or increase profits."

The president of an Indiana corporation mentioned that he was looking for what the applicant had accomplished, not just the years at each job and the title of the position.

Effective or ineffective? Remember, you have about twenty seconds to sell yourself—that's the time it generally takes for an employer to scan and then read a resume if it has caught her attention. An effective resume does not require the reader to work hard to figure out what you have that might be valuable to her. She doesn't have to make the translation between your past and your future. You do the translation for her. The bottom line is this: You want someone to read your resume and then want to meet you. Or if she has met you, you want your resume to accurately reflect the interaction she had when she met you. You want such a strong resume that even if your resume is received in the final stages of a search, it stimulates reopening the search.

Is there such a thing as an ideal resume? No. However, the most effective resumes are ones that sell ability and talent rather than just experience. The more your background is projected as a series of potential benefits substantiated by actual accomplishments, the easier your job search will become. And remember, successful job changers never underestimate their achievements.

Executives in the employment field say that the best resume is one that presents the key facts enabling them to make a quick decision. The idea is to think carefully about anything you have done that makes you feel good about yourself. When a prospective employer looks at your resume, you want her to think of you as someone who can save the company money and time.

When you consider sending a resume to an employer, focus on answering the company's number one question: "What can you do for us?" You can't be there to answer the question, so your resume must speak for you.

Which Format?

Which is the best format to use for a resume? Opinions vary, but don't get confused. Each resume style actually contains the same information: employment history, education, skills, accomplishments, and objectives. It's just the presentation of the data that differs.

You may need to consider using more than one format to tailor different resumes for different types of jobs and industries. One resume "shotgunned" in response to every ad or job possibility may not get the results desired, especially if you are a multitalented person. Computers make it easy to change a few words or rephrase a summary, even though the basic resume itself remains intact.

A *targeted* resume sells you more efficiently because it deliberately positions you for a specific job as you zero in on the objective(s) specified in an ad. This may take more time and effort but in all probability will "sell" you much more advantageously. Remember, your goal is to construct an effective means of selling your way into an interview. (This can also be done in a very good cover letter.) "Always think in terms of the market you are hoping to move into," advises the president of a professional writing service.

If you are using a professional resume writer, you can do some targeting if you are willing to pay an additional fee. This shouldn't be an exorbitant amount or take very long since the operator can store your resume for you and simply type in whatever new information is required. More than likely this would be at the top of the resume in the Objective and/or Summary statements.

As for the Objective, simply tell what job you are seeking. It might be very specific (e.g., director of marketing) or more general (e.g., middle-management position in marketing). List the position(s) you are capable of filling, but keep it brief.

A Summary statement should also be to the point, stating what you have done to qualify for the job objective (e.g., "Over twenty years' professional experience as a marketing generalist with a strong background in planning, forecasting, market research, and product development").

You may choose to combine the Objective and Summary statements using the one word *Objective.*

The Chronological Resume

Sometimes called the historical resume format, the chronological resume is the most common presentation. Employment professionals estimate that two-thirds of resumes are in the chronological style. It is traditionally used by managers and professionals whose careers have had an unbroken succession of increasingly responsible positions. It is a natural way to show how you have steadily climbed the ladder in a single field, and it can be very advantageous in showcasing your accomplishments.

In this format the words *Work Experience* or *Professional Experience* are used as the heading following your Objective statement. You could capitalize these words followed by a colon. Indented two spaces under this you begin your career summary with your current or most recent employment and continue backwards. List the job title, then the company name, the dates you held each job, and a brief description of your responsibilities.

To make your resume even more effective, summarize your specific achievements under each of these positions in a way that focuses on the employer to whom you are applying. Make the person scanning the resume realize that your achievements would be a transferable skill into the company (e.g., "Increased market share by 2 percent, or $5 million"). Make these achievement statements hard-hitting, using action verbs and showing the value of your work to the employer.

Your recent achievements will be of the most interest to a prospective employer, so the further you go into the past, the less information you will include. If you are a mature job seeker with a long work history, you may want to use the functional resume (see next section).

The chronological format is easy to read, which in itself is a plus. But it does have a drawback, working against you if your work history is ragged. If you have changed jobs too often, you will come across as a job hopper. Short tenures or any major gaps in employment history will be noticed as well. Rather than showing months of employment, you may want to provide just the year. Be careful lest you prematurely remove yourself from consideration with one careless entry on your resume.

Leaving some points out of your resume is not lying. We all make mistakes in our professional lives, so there is no sense in flagging them. "Tell the truth—fine," Kenneth and Sheryl Dawson say in *Job Search: The Total System.* "But don't look for a job the way a kamikaze pilot flies an airplane. If the information will hurt you, leave it out of your resume. Period. That's not a lie."[4]

The Functional Resume

The functional resume is the best format for those who have done part-time work or have limited work experience. If you have been a career switcher, this kind of resume ignores chronological order and downplays or omits dates. It can even omit employers' names and job titles. Others who find this resume best are those who are reentering the workforce after many years of being away (e.g., homemakers, widows, or recently divorced women). People who have experienced prolonged unemployment can also benefit from the functional format.

This format directs the reader's attention to transferable functional skills by grouping several different accomplishments under one area of expertise. The accomplishments, therefore, don't necessarily have to be work related. You can use examples from volunteerism, school, and other nonwork activities.

The functional resume allows you to bypass the problems of little or no formal work experience by concentrating on the knowledge you have acquired. Don't minimize this. Life experiences count for something and are excellent tools for use in the work world. Highlight your skills and accomplishments rather than paying homage to time periods. You don't have to feature when and where you learned to do something.

This format is a good way to maximize strengths if you have held a number of jobs, are a mature job seeker, or fit into any of the categories mentioned earlier. It focuses on the marketing strategy of instant reader attention, and that's not bad.

The downside to functional resumes is that many employers red-flag them, believing that their writers are trying to hide something or cover up a weak employment background. Personnel managers are more accustomed to a chronological presentation of work history, so departing from the norm can raise suspicion. Keep that in mind if you choose to use this format.

The Chronological/Functional Format

Sometimes called the basic combination resume or hybrid resume, the chronological/functional format is exactly what the name implies—it uses elements of both the chronological and functional formats. This is a popular resume style, frequently recommended in current articles by many savvy career counselors.

The bulk of a combination resume is functional. It organizes your background by skills and function rather than job title. Use the heading Skills followed by a colon. The next line, indented, should identify those skills (e.g., Public Relations [then highlighting notable achievements in three or four strong statements]; Television [the same highlighting of accomplishments in bullet statements]; and Administration [mention administrative accomplishments on any or all of your positions]).

This section is followed by the section Experience, under which you would provide a list of job titles and companies in reverse chronological order.

This is the resume of choice for many job seekers because it does a great job of presenting what you can do while at the same time overcoming doubts in the minds of readers by providing documentation of your background.

Whatever your format choice, your resume should conclude with a brief summation of your education and outside activities (in particular, memberships in professional organizations and/or civic involvement). Also include any professional awards or honors received. If you have written any articles or books, list them here. Make certain that your list reflects positive characteristics. Stay away from mentioning groups that would be considered overtly political or controversial.

Regarding education, list the school(s) you attended, degree(s) earned, year(s) in which you earned your degree(s), major, and any honors. If you have been out of school for some time, the rule of thumb is that it should take up very little space on your resume. If you are a recent graduate or still a student, expand the education section, especially if it will enhance your candidacy for the position.

It is not necessary to add the statement: "References available upon request." It is assumed that you can provide such references if you are asked to do so. There are six basic guidelines to remember when writing a resume:

1. Be brief (consolidate information).
2. Be specific (provide concrete examples of achievements rather than writing in vague generalities).
3. Be active (strong words that show action).
4. Be selective (target yourself precisely).
5. Be honest.
6. Be consistent in spacing between lines, headers, font size, text justification, punctuation, and use of formatting such as bold and italics. (Consistency will make your resume easier to read and show that you are detail oriented.)

Make certain before you write a resume or seek professional help that you have uncovered every conceivable asset, skill, or work experience that might help you sell yourself. In essence, your resume becomes your personal career history database, and it will save you much trial and error in the marketplace. Your marketable strengths, transferable skills, and any other personal attributes are critical to your success. If you have done this, you are going to look great on that resume.

Psalm 138:8 says, "The LORD will perfect that which concerns me." This has proven true for countless numbers of job seekers, and it can prove true for you too.

11

Writing to Influence

Never underestimate the potential of a well-written, good old-fashioned letter in seeking to become employed. Writing such a letter just might achieve a breakthrough for you that nothing else has achieved.

Letter writing is fast becoming a lost art. Most people don't like to write letters or complain that it takes too much time. All kinds of excuses can be found for not disciplining oneself to apply the seat of the anatomy to the seat of a chair to write letters.

But if you are going to conduct a successful job search, you can't get away from it. You are going to have to send letters either with resumes or, in some instances, alone as an introduction, hoping to get your foot in the door for an interview. As Robert Louis Stevenson aptly observed, the difficulty is not just to affect your reader, but to affect him precisely as you wish. While it is true that positions have been obtained without the use of a job search letter, the importance of a well-crafted cover letter must not be minimized. It most definitely will enhance the likelihood of results.

Regardless of how you feel about writing, it is never too late to develop this skill. Contrary to popular opinion, I believe good writers are made. Writing is a process to be practiced and mastered.

One of the things I observed in reading the classified ads from various cities as I did research at the library was the emphasis on employers wanting people with "good communication skills" in jobs ranging from clerical workers to hospital administrators. The *Chicago Tribune* had a feature article entitled "Wanted: People Who Can Write, Speak, Listen." The article explained that just a decade ago, top employers looked for workers with good technical skills, but in today's market that is not enough.

The plethora of information that must be communicated makes the old arts of writing, speaking, and listening work necessities and a part of many job descriptions. "These attributes are referred to by human resource managers as 'good communication skills,' and the phrase has become an employment buzzword," the article stated. Good communication skills have literally become a requirement in the twenty-first-century job market, as necessary for engineers as for sales personnel, as essential for support staff as for supervisors.

Why has this happened? According to a senior-level executive search firm in San Francisco, "With the increasing problems of public education and the high rate of illiteracy in the nation, employers more and more are asking for people with good communication skills."

So communicate you must. Do it superbly and you are almost guaranteed a job interview. *Always* write a cover letter when you send out a resume. Cold resumes unaccompanied by a letter almost always land in the nearest round file (i.e., wastebasket). Anyone who sends a resume to a company without a well-written cover letter stands very little chance of being called in for an interview, especially in today's tight labor market.

Writing counts, and it just might achieve a breakthrough for you. Treat a prospective employer almost like you would a lover. That is, let him know you've been thinking about him, that his company is great, that it matters a lot that you get together.

Write So the Receiver Will Enjoy Your Letter

When putting together your cover letter, use good sense and be tasteful. You are writing to a complete stranger who can give you an opportunity for an interview or turn you away. Don't be too familiar. Avoid sounding unduly cozy or colloquial. Your letter shouldn't sound like a neighbor gossiping over the back fence. On the other hand, don't be too stuffy and come off sounding like a pompous know-it-all. Employers like to be courted and admired like anyone else. Your objective should be to establish a relationship and build a bridge to a meeting.

William Zinsser, in *On Writing Well*, asks, "Who is this elusive creature the reader?" and answers by telling us he is a person with an attention span of about twenty seconds. He's assailed on every side by forces competing for his time.[1]

The late Malcolm Forbes was asked how to write a business letter. "People who read business letters are as human as thee and me," he said. "Reading a letter shouldn't be a chore—*reward* the reader for the time he gives you. Write so he'll enjoy it. Write the entire letter from his point of view—what's in it for *him*? Beat him to the draw—surprise him by answering the questions and objections he might have."

He underscored the need to be positive, nice, and natural. "Don't be cute or flippant," he warned. "This doesn't mean you've got to be dull. You prefer your letter to knock 'em dead rather than bore 'em to death."

Kathryn and Ross Petras, in *The Only Job Hunting Guide You'll Ever Need*, give this advice for targeting your reader:

> Create a mental image of your reader. Whether your image of the individual to whom you're writing is a correct one or not is immaterial. Use it simply as a device to make your letter more personal rather than dry and dull. You can base your mental image on what you know of the industry and the people in it—anything that will help you get a fix on the type of person you're trying to reach through your letter.[2]

How can you capture the reader's attention so that he attaches a memo to your letter that reads, "Call this person in for an interview"? How can you come across as not sounding too unconcerned or too desperate, too meek or too aggressive, too self-confident or too timid?

Forbes suggests three things:

1. Have a sense of humor (be refreshing).
2. Be specific (give the reader something to sink his teeth into).
3. Lean heavier on nouns and verbs, lighter on adjectives. Use the active voice instead of the passive. "Your writing will have more guts."

Merchandise Your Talents

Remember what you learned earlier? You have to market yourself. This letter is another facet of your sales presentation. Think about the prospective employer as the receiver and you, the sender, as the product or service offered. How can you present yourself as an irresistible product? How can you distinguish yourself from the pack?

Since style is who you are, the secret is to be true to yourself. "Relax and say what you want to say," advises Zinsser. "Whatever your age, be yourself when you write."[3]

"Write the way you feel it," I often tell aspiring writers, "and write the way you talk." (Hopefully, you talk well!) "Sound like yourself," urges best-selling author Kurt Vonnegut.

How can you apply this advice to writing your job-search letter?

The Challenge: Getting the Reader's Attention

When it comes to writing letters, research pays off. You can gain leverage by knowing something about the company to which you are applying. Moreover, you can target your letter to a specific individual so that it isn't just a "To whom it may concern" impersonal letter. It will concern no one if you don't personalize it.

Malcolm Forbes says to plunge right in and call the person by name—and be sure to spell it right. (Usually you can accomplish this by phoning the company or consulting a business directory at the library, such as *The Standard & Poor's Register* or *The Dun & Bradstreet Directory*.)

I made my greatest inroads in attracting favorable attention by the targeted letters I wrote. For instance, using the database information supplied by my career counselor, I researched the broad health care field and sent a letter to the CEO at a northern California hospital I had read about in a Sacramento paper. I commented about the growth, the new additions to the hospital, and the projected plans for the future. I congratulated him for his role in what was taking place. Then I introduced myself with bulleted statements highlighting accomplishments and how I envisioned my skills making valuable contributions to the hospital's needs.

Within a few days he replied. He thanked me for the "warm letter," for my "kind comments" to him personally, and stated how impressed he was that I had studied what was taking place at the hospital. He regretted that they were fully staffed but assured me that my letter and resume would be kept where they could be accessed easily. He invited me to stop by the hospital to meet him personally whenever I was in the city.

Making contact with this hospital was tapping what is commonly called "the hidden job market." Though they hadn't advertised, my research revealed that they were a progressive, growth-oriented organization. I took a chance, but for whatever my experience is worth, I received more responses from such job-search efforts than anything else I did. The sources I used in my research, for the most part, pointed out that the most consistently effective way for anyone to generate interviews is through direct mail to executives.

In another instance a similar letter to a CEO resulted in an invitation to stop by at my convenience to meet with the human resource director. I called in advance, made an appointment, and had an hour-long visit that blossomed into an ongoing friendship. I was asked to stay in touch because a position appropriate to my background and career interests was in the talking stages and might develop in the near future.

In my original letter I had commented about the CEO's entrepreneurial spirit, that reading about him had captivated my attention because I likewise was an entrepreneur at heart (having founded two book and gift shops at one time in Southern California). These kinds of statements are literally door openers. Use them, linking your background, interests, and experience to what you unearth in your research.

Another time the human resources manager of a nationally known magazine published in northern California called in response to a letter I'd written to the publisher. "Mr. ___ would like to meet you," she said. I spent the morning, in fact, with this highly respected gentleman. And though there were no job openings (they'd had severe cutbacks and were on a hiring freeze), my letter had caught his attention.

The challenge for you is to find the "hook," as it were, that you can hang your letter on and then give it your best. Your skills and unique qualities are that hook. Knowledge about the individual or organization to which you are writing, and then referencing your own experience to what they have to offer, will work for your benefit and can result in an interview and a mutually profitable discussion.

Deborah Dumaine, in *Write to the Top: Writing for Corporate Success*, emphasizes the need to take a positive approach in writing. She explains that sometimes your tone carries a hidden message to the reader, that between the lines you communicate your self-confidence or self-doubt. Ideas expressed positively are most likely to be positively received by the reader. To get the results you desire, you must convey an attitude of confident expectation.[4]

William Zinsser, in his classic book, *On Writing Well*, says that leaders who bob and weave like aging boxers don't inspire confidence—or deserve it. The same thing is true of writers. Sell yourself, and your subject will exert its own appeal. Believe in your own identity and your own opinions. Proceed with confidence, generating it, if necessary, by pure willpower. Writing is an act of ego and you might as well admit it. Use its energy to keep yourself going.[5]

Perhaps you are thinking, *I'm not a writer. I just can't write that kind of letter.* Good, clear writing is the result of attention and care. And it does take time. Since time is of the essence when you are unemployed, you may want to get the help of a professional. Resume writers also compose letters for their clients, or you may enlist the help of a friend or family member.

Once you have crafted a basic letter, you can use it over and over again just by changing the components to reflect the company to which you are writing and highlighting different parts of your background that are especially applicable to the position for which you are applying.

Putting Your Best Foot Forward

Your letter is a stand-in for you. Pretend you are sitting across from the person to whom you are writing. Talk to that person; be natural. Give your best.

When you meet someone for the first time, what is it that makes you warm up to him or her or turns you off altogether? While writing this I met the creator of the Biblical Wreath, a beautiful creation composed of dried plants, flowers, herbs, buds, fruits, and nuts representing foliage found in the Holy Land. It was awesome. Standing in front of it in a charming, historically significant, mill turned art gallery (called Country Mates) in the lakefront community of New Buffalo, Michigan, I turned and saw the artist. Immediately I expressed admiration. "I'm *so* moved," I said. "Wreaths—I've seen all kinds, but this . . . this is *so* meaningful . . ." We had instant rapport.

"But that's different," you might protest. "He was right there. It was obviously something you could admire." Wait, just a moment. You are seeking to gain rapport with the person to whom you are writing. Obviously he is an accomplished person to have reached the position of authority he is in. What stands out? What is it the company has done that makes it attractive to you? A positive, complimentary truism about the company's or an individual's performance works. Just don't gush.

Undeniably, you are appealing to the ego of the person to whom you are writing. There is nothing wrong with that as long as it is a genuine compliment or acknowledgment. You don't want to come across as a professional hype artist. Perhaps he or she has been quoted in a newspaper or magazine or has been interviewed on TV. Maybe the business section of the Sunday paper contained a photo and a reference to a recent promotion or something significant that has taken place at the company. Have your antenna up, watch for these things, latch on to them, and use them as leaders in your letter.

To capture the reader's attention, create a visual design in your letter that entices him. Make your letter look appetizing. You want the letter to be easy to read with key points jumping out. That's called effective visual impact. You can accomplish this by

1. keeping paragraphs short;
2. using bulleted statements (a little black circle [•] to the left of an indented statement);
3. underlining for emphasis where you want a date or statement to stand out (use sparingly in letters, however);
4. keeping the letter to one page if at all possible.

At the end of this chapter, I have included several examples of cover letters to help you get started.

Helpful Guidelines

Choose your words carefully. When you are choosing words and stringing them together, bear in mind how they sound. That may seem absurd; after all, readers read with their eyes, don't they? Yes, but they hear what they are reading in their inner ear far more than you realize. Think in terms of rhythm and alliteration for every sentence. Read your letter out loud, and you will see what I mean. Ask yourself if it sounds respectful, informative, and straightforward. Is it easy to read?

Zinsser reminds his readers, "Remember that words are the only tools that you will be given. Learn to use them with originality and care. Value them for their strength and their infinite diversity. And also remember: Somebody out there is listening."[6]

Be concise. Make every word count. Say what you have to say and then, as someone has said so pointedly, "Shut up!" If you do this, your letters will have energy and focus, and, most importantly, they will get read. Good writing has an aliveness to it that gets noticed and keeps the reader going from one paragraph to the next. Edit ruthlessly. If you can't be objective about your own literary masterpiece, ask for help.

Clutter is the disease of American writing. We are a society strangling in unnecessary words and meaningless jargon. The secret of good writing is to strip every sentence to its cleanest components, reminds Zinsser. He points to Thoreau, who said, "Simplify, simplify."

How can this be accomplished? Think with your thinker. Ernest Hemingway said, "I think a lot and write very little."

"The answer is to clear our heads of clutter," says Zinsser. "Clutter is the enemy, whatever form it takes. It slows the reader and robs the writer of his personality, making him seem pretentious." Zinsser likens wordiness, jargon, and long words to weeds that smother what you write. He also speaks of them as being bloated monsters that lie in ambush for the writer trying to put together a clean English sentence. Be crystal clear. Clear thinking becomes clear writing. It is impossible for a muddy thinker to write good English.[7]

Keep your language down-to-earth. Use short sentences, short paragraphs, and simple but powerful words. You don't have to exaggerate or use obscure words. The reader will sense it if you are putting on airs. Pretense invariably impresses only the pretender. You want to come across as someone who is genuine.

Check your spelling, punctuation, and grammar. Proofread what you write. It has to be perfect. That means no typos, no misspellings, no factual errors. Avoid contractions.

Do you know what the cost of a misspelled word is? Research shows that the main cost is psychological. To most people, misspelled words indicate a lack of competence and intelligence.

Organize your letter. Think of your letter as needing to have three basic parts:

1. *The introduction.* State in the introduction who you are and why you are writing (the purpose). If you are writing in response to an ad, say so. If you are writing because of your research or something you read in a business journal, newsletter, or elsewhere, explain. Demonstrate the level of your interest by showing the reader that you are knowledgeable about the corporation.

2. *The sales pitch.* In the second part of the letter, use facts and numbers to demonstrate why this company should hire you. The recipient of your letter will primarily want to know, "What can this person do for us?" So use bullet statements with active verbs to direct the reader's attention to your strong points. List new targeted statements that aren't in your resume. If you use the exact wording that is in your resume, your cover letter will seem redundant. If you are writing in response to an ad, it is very important that you match your statements to the ad's specifications.

Don't just give a bland recitation of your work history; reinforce your achievements. Strive to communicate your message clearly.

If the ad requests applicants' salary requirements, give a salary range, adding the words, "depending on the nature and scope of duties and responsibilities," or a phrase to that effect. The overall ironclad rule is if the ad doesn't mention salary requirements, don't you either. Why give another excuse for getting your response screened out?

175

3. *The close.* Great is the art of beginning, said Longfellow, but greater is the art of ending. So make your closing memorable. You've just made a strong case for yourself, so now is the time to leave the reader wanting to learn more by meeting you. Use a proactive statement; take the initiative for the next contact. Aim for an interview with the reader. For example, "I'll call the week of May 10 to see if we can arrange a mutually convenient time to meet." This is called being professionally assertive. (You would not use this, however, in response to an ad.)

You may be uncomfortable using such an assertive approach. If so, restate your interest in working with a company such as theirs, and seek to come across as being genuinely enthusiastic. Don't oversell yourself in your close.

Malcolm Forbes says to sum it up and get out. The last paragraph should tell the reader exactly what you want *him* or *her* to do, or what *you're* going to do. Short and sweet.

Kenneth and Sheryl Dawson recommend adding a fourth section to a letter, calling it their "favorite innovation." "Save your one grand slam accomplishment to mention in a P.S.," they say, pointing to studies of business letters that prove conclusively that the segment of a letter that is most often read and retained is the first sentence, and the second most read is a postscript.[8]

Resume Alternative: The Broadcast Letter

David R. Kessler, in *Job Seekers Handbook*, suggests using a broadcast letter technique as a resume alternative. Such a letter focuses only on your personal achievements and accomplishments. The idea is to paint a vivid, concrete picture of your successes. You are fashioning a direct-mail piece to sell your strengths, targeting a certain occupation or industry. Stress only those things you consider to be the high points of your life or the major accomplishments in your career. Achievements are the things that ultimately make a big difference in helping you get in the door for an interview.

Four approaches can be used most effectively in a broadcast letter. Variation on these could also be used in constructing a cover letter to accompany a resume.

1. *The accomplishment approach.* Start your letter with a statement that will get the recipient's attention and encourage him to read on (e.g., "As the number two salesperson on a ten-member team, I have gained years of experience in developing rapport with prospective customers, and I have a thorough understanding of what can be achieved through hard work").

It should be noted that accomplishments don't necessarily have to be something you did entirely on your own. It is also important to remember that accomplishments should always be quantifiable in terms of numbers, percentages, hours, or dollars.

The idea is to be creative and include examples of things that set you apart. How did you save a company money or time or make a difference in some significant way?

2. *The referral approach.* In the referral approach you take advantage of knowing someone who carries some weight with the reader. Here is where networking counts. Of course you will need to make certain the person you are referring to gives permission for you to do this.

Also, be sure the person you are contacting thinks highly of your referral (e.g., "According to John Bell, you are currently looking for a sales professional to fill an opening in your leasing department").

3. *The philosophical approach.* The philosophical approach requires that you use your personal beliefs in the hopes of hitting some hot buttons and gaining favorable attention. This would work well in seeking employment with nonprofit, religious, charitable, or even political organizations. You would need to know the set of beliefs held

by the person or organization to whom you are directing your efforts.

For instance, if you are hoping to become affiliated with a group that has strong sentiments on the abortion issue and you hold those same beliefs, you should find it relatively easy to compose a strong letter. But a word of caution is in order. You don't want to come across as being offensive, rigid, or controversial. You should be able to state your personal philosophy and use concepts that are not likely to be contested. Always be prepared to back up your beliefs in an interview.

Depending on your approach, this could be very effective, or you could find yourself "dead in the water." This is an approach you should weigh very carefully, because it could either work marvelously in your favor or cause your first impression to hit with a thud.

4. *The startling statement approach*. Using a startling statement is a fun approach with which you can be completely creative. Open your letter with a relevant statement that helps make your point. For instance, you could quote someone well-known whose name would carry weight, or you could use one of your own unique statements. Use caution with this approach or you could come off looking like you lack taste or even common sense! If you're careful, you just might make your letter unique enough to get noticed.

Here are a couple of ideas:

- Lee Iacocca said he liked working with people more than machines. So do I . . .
- "The difference between mediocrity and greatness is the feeling the guys [on the football team] have for each other. Most people call it team spirit. When the players are imbued with that special feeling, you know you've got yourself a winning team," Vince Lombardi said. I couldn't agree more. The same principle applies in the work world. I consider myself a team player . . .

The Conclusion of the Matter

An old proverb says nothing is to be gained without pain. Writing is work, often a painful process requiring many hours of toil. But the effort you put forth will be worth it, for as another proverb says, the pen is mightier than the sword. And you can get into a person's office via a letter when you can't get in any other way.

Think of the writing process using the acronym, POWER.

P   Plan
O   Organize
W   Write
E   Edit
R   Rewrite

Sample Cover Letter #1: Answering an Ad

Dear Mr. Bell:

Telephonic's accomplishments during the last several years have not gone unnoticed by me. For that reason, your ad in last week's *National Business Employment Weekly* for a director of marketing communications caught my attention. The position sounds very interesting and matches my career objectives.

As the enclosed resume shows, I have a proven record of success in communications and public relations. Those qualifications that I would like to bring to your attention include:

- Managed budgets from $50,000 to $5 million.
- Created and produced award-winning videos and communications material.
- Established cost-effective use of outside vendors.

179

- Coordinated promotional and media events, including annual conventions and trade shows in Dallas, Anaheim, Seattle, and Atlanta.
- Obtained worldwide press coverage.
- Developed programs and collateral material that were delivered on time, within budget, and met all marketing objectives.

I would value an opportunity to meet with you to discuss this position. Working with your organization would be a challenge I would not regard lightly.

If you have any questions or would like to call and arrange an interview, I can be reached at (555) 555-5555. Thank you very kindly for your consideration.

Sincerely,

Lee Jones

Enclosure

The bullets in the preceding letter match the specific requirements of a hypothetical ad. The objective is to predispose the reader to appreciate those parts of the resume that are relevant to the position advertised.

Another format that can be used effectively is to list the position criteria from the ad on the left side of the page and specific accomplishments or information from your background and experience on the right.

Sample Cover Letter #2: Answering an Ad

Dear Mr. Bell:

Telephonic's accomplishments during the last several years have not gone unnoticed by me. For that reason, your ad in last week's *National Business Employment Weekly* for a director of marketing communications caught my attention. The position

180

sounds very interesting and matches my career objectives.

As the enclosed resume shows, I have a proven record of success in communications and public relations. I highlighted below some relevant experience that matches your position criteria:

Position Criteria   Relevant Experience
[List the criteria   [List your
from the ad]   experience that
                           matches]

[Conclude your letter . . .]

Sample Cover Letter #3: Targeting a Company

Dear Mr. Zee:

Your interview on Channel 67 last Thursday prompted me to write this letter. [You could refer to a newspaper or magazine article about him or the company.] Your comments regarding the use of media and marketing in the twenty-first century were well stated and reflect my own sentiments. If you are searching for an experienced marketing communications professional or contemplating this in the near future, then please take a moment to consider the following:

- Managed budgets from $50,000 to $5 million.
- Created and produced award-winning videos and communications material.
- Established cost-effective use of outside vendors.
- Coordinated promotional and media events, including annual conventions and trade shows in Dallas, Anaheim, Seattle, and Atlanta.
- Obtained worldwide press coverage.
- Developed programs and collateral material that were delivered on time, within budget, and met all marketing objectives.

I would value an opportunity to meet with you to discuss this position. Working with your organization would be a challenge I would not regard lightly. I will call in a few days after you have had an opportunity to review the enclosed resume.

If you have any questions or would like to call and arrange an interview, I can be reached at (555) 555-5555. Thank you very kindly for your consideration.

Sincerely,

Lee Jones

Enclosure

———⊰⊱———

Below you will find possible opening scenarios you can use to utilize your research and match your credentials to what you have learned.

Sample Cover Letter #4: Targeting a Company

Dear Ms. Otis:

Congratulations on the expansion of your advertising agency. The story in *Advertising Weekly* portrays a company whose future looks bright indeed. Your record and achievements are impressive.

I am convinced that I want to become a part of an organization that is on the move like this. I would like to persuade you to give me an opportunity to present my credentials in detail. At this time there are a few salient points about me that I will include with this letter.

[Then use three or four bulleted statements highlighting your achievements.]

Dear Mr. Fine:

Does Fine & Company need an account executive with experience that has contributed to a sales growth of 249 percent and a profit growth of 322 percent? Such percentages may seem astounding, but they did occur as my current employer grew from $7.5 million in sales to over $50 million.

[Then launch into highlighting your achievements with your bullet statements.]

Sample Cover Letter #5: To an Association or Organization of Which You Are a Member

Dear Ms. Helpful:

As a fellow member of the Association of Women Accountants, I am writing to ask for your help.

As the enclosed resume indicates, I am an experienced certified public accountant who has demonstrated success in our field. I am presently launching a job search in the greater Los Angeles area. Understandably, you can appreciate that it is impossible for me to be aware of every position that might be out there. With this in mind, I am simply asking that you take a moment to review the resume I have enclosed and possibly provide names and addresses of people and/or companies you feel I should be talking to.

Any suggestions you can make to help me in my job search would be greatly appreciated. Perhaps you can direct me to others within our association who might be of assistance. Obviously, the more people I can talk to in this endeavor, the better my chances are of uncovering just the position I am seeking.

Again, I appreciate your taking the time to help me with my efforts. I will be contacting you in a week or so to gather any ideas you might have.

Thank you very kindly for your assistance.

Sincerely,

Margaret Thompson

Enclosure

Sample Cover Letter #6: To Recruiters

Dear Mr. Available:

Your firm has come to my attention as one that frequently conducts client searches for marketing professionals with solid credentials and experience in advertising, promotions, and public relations. Please take a moment to consider the following:

[bulleted statements]

Confident that my experience, strengths, and skills are transferable into a broad range of environments, I am interested in exploring situations and opportunities in a variety of industries.

If there are any questions or additional information you need, please call me at (555) 555-5555. I would value an opportunity to meet with you. Thank you for your assistance.

Sincerely,

Peter Hall

P.S. I will call in another week if I haven't heard from you to see if there is a mutually convenient date that we could meet.

Enclosure

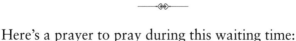

Here's a prayer to pray during this waiting time:

Father, teach me to wait patiently in the very inaction of this present time. Waiting is hard. Our circumstances grow more difficult, it seems, with each passing day. Strengthen me and provide direction and discernment. Help me to understand

184

that you are working in my behalf. Thank you for the encouragement of your Word and friends and family who care. Thank you for the answer that I know is coming. Amen.

When I cannot understand my Father's leading, and it seems to be but hard and cruel fate, still I hear that gentle whisper ever pleading, God is working, God is faithful, *only wait.*

12

The Job Interview

Whether you're interviewing for a position as a banker, an astronaut or a sewer worker, interviewers want to know about three basic things: your experience, your interpersonal skills, and the reasons they should hire you.

Kathryn and Ross Petras, *The Only Job Hunting Guide You'll Ever Need*

The former governor of Kentucky, John Y. Brown, is credited with saying, "I have never seen a bad resume." Harvey Mackay, author of *Swim with the Sharks without Being Eaten* and called "Mr. Make-Things-Happen" by *Fortune* magazine, refers to Brown's statement, adding, "The former governor's wry observation should be tattooed on every manager's forehead."

Everybody's a winner. It's in the flesh that the differences stand out. Who would have hired failed haberdasher Harry S. Truman based on a resume, or chosen seventy-three-year-

187

old Eureka College graduate Ronald Reagan over Walter Mondale, a polished lawyer, after comparing their paper credentials? Hiring the right people is the greatest talent a manager can have, because good people produce good work and lousy people do lousy work.[1]

Lee Iacocca had this to say about interviewees:

There are two really important things about a candidate that you just can't learn from one short job interview. The first is whether he's lazy, and the second is whether he's got any horse sense. There's no qualitative analysis to check out whether he's got some fire in his belly, or whether he will have savvy—or street smarts—when it comes to decision time.[2]

You "in the Flesh"

How can you come across as being one of those "good people" Mackay refers to? Is there some way for the interviewer to sense that you have savvy, street smarts, and horse sense? How can you let him or her know that you're not lazy and that there is "fire in your belly"?

Kenneth and Sheryl Dawson say that a job interview is not an exchange of information but a psychological tennis match: "Your task is to hold your serve by controlling—very subtly—the direction of the interview." Successful interviewing is an art form, a performance. They teach their clients that they must approach an interview as though they were contestants in a beauty pageant or a dog and pony show. "In business terminology, visualize it as a sales call," they say. They point out that some people resist these kinds of analogies, but the truth is job hunters fail or succeed according to their ability to grasp the reality of the scenario and turn it to their advantage. The first rule to keep in mind in any interview is this: *Give them a reason to want you.*[3]

Ask yourself these questions: How can I stand out from all the other applicants for this position? How can I distinguish myself from the rest of the competition? What ideas can I put in this interviewer's head that she will chew on later and remember when it comes time to make a decision? Richard Bolles points out that if you understand what an interview is, you will be ahead of 98 percent of all other job hunters who go into the interview as a lamb goes to the slaughter.

Whatever type of interview you're having, your strategy should be the same—to sell your way into a job. There are only two parts to an interview: the first five minutes and the rest.

Here's a winning formula for most interviews:

- Make a good first impression.
- Have a sincere, enthusiastic nature.
- Use a warm smile.
- Display an interesting personality.
- Articulate answers to interview questions.
- Ask well-thought-out questions of your own.
- Project a high energy level and a dedication to achievement.

Since it is generally conceded that 70 percent of a job search is marketing—how you communicate your skills and how you come across as a person—it is of utmost importance that you put your best foot forward. The rest of this chapter will provide clues as to how to go about this.

Kathryn and Ross Petras say in *The Only Job Hunting Guide You'll Ever Need*, "In the first five minutes you should sell your attitude and personality. Show you're a winner by your stance, your confidence, and your demeanor. During the rest of the interview you should prove how the interviewer's first impression of you is correct. Highlight your skills and background and why you are right for this job."[4]

What Petras, the Dawsons, and other experts are emphasizing is that we need to go into an interview prepared. This will ensure that there are no embarrassing pauses in the conversation when being asked questions. We won't have to take time to reflect on how best to answer, nor stammer and wade through an emotional response, fighting to control ourselves.

Underscore this in your thinking: *you are selling and marketing yourself.* You are the commodity. A decision is going to be made whether to "buy or not to buy" your skills and experience. Self-marketing is the name of the game. That's what you did on your resume; now you have the opportunity to wrap up the sale in person.

Your statements in the interview should be an amplification of what appears on your resume, not simply a rehash. Use well-thought-out, credible statements, not inflated or exaggerated answers to questions. Concentrate on what your research and preparation have indicated this particular company is looking for.

Someone has said that you can get a job without a resume, but you can't get a job without an interview. Interestingly enough, most people don't talk enough during an interview. Instead of taking charge of selling themselves, they allow the interviewer to ask all the questions and content themselves with just answering them. They *respond*; they don't initiate.

Job interviews are two-way exchanges: you should be as interested in making sure that the job is right for you as the interviewer will be in whether you are right for the job. Preparing questions of your own about duties and policies allows you to make an informed decision and shows you are interested. Studies reveal that the people who get hired are those who mix speaking and listening fifty-fifty in the interview. That is, half the time you listen while the interviewer talks, the other half you talk.

A word of caution is necessary, however. You need to convey an image of professionalism and not come across as being dominant, aggressive, or rude in striving to participate in the interview. Just remember that an interview, like a sales call, requires your active participation in establishing a dialogue. You don't just want to be interviewed. That is much too passive. Avoid sitting there like a bump on a log, expecting the interviewer to be impressed by your sweet demeanor.

Words can get you hired as well as fired. Ultimately, among applicants of equal ability, what any successful interview comes down to is giving the right answers to the right questions. "What you want to do is simply highlight your strong points," advises a vice president of an outplacement firm engaged to coach severed employees in job-finding techniques.

"Almost anyone can learn to carry off a good interview," claims a Kansas City outplacement consultant. "You may not be a salesperson, but you have a huge advantage. You know the product—yourself—better than anyone else."

Some people role-play the interview using a mirror, a home video recorder, a tape recorder, or a friend or family member. When you watch the video or listen to the recording, ask yourself, *Would I hire this person?* If you have someone role-playing with you, assure him he will be doing you no favor if he isn't honest with you. After all you have been through in being unemployed, you have developed tough skin. (You will quickly figure out who your real friends are.)

Make Body Language Work for You

This is a good place to point out that body language can be made to work for you. We choose our words carefully to convey just the right message in an interview, but many of us don't give as much thought to the messages we send without words. Gestures, speaking style, and appearance are valuable communication tools. These nonverbal cues tell a lot about what people really are feeling.

Are you aware that studies show that 65 to 90 percent of all communication is nonverbal? Body language can help you communicate clearly, accurately, vibrantly, and with credibility. This includes movement, facial expressions, posture, use of silence, use of touch, timing, distance between speakers and listeners, physical surroundings, tone, and rhythm of speech.

You will want to make sure your body language matches your verbal message. Astute listeners (interviewers) will pick up on inconsistencies. Often we send out nonverbal cues of which we aren't even aware. For example, some people touch too much, or they wear a constant, insincere smile. Sometimes we use our hands inappropriately. Eliminate irrelevant, distracting gestures, such as fidgeting, picking at your fingers, or doodling. And be sure not to sit sternly with your arms folded across your chest.

Do use eye contact. Don't stare, but maintain a steady gaze aimed at the other person's eyes and face. Good eye contact signals that you think the other person is important and that you are a cooperative person. Used wrongly, it may signal dominance and assertiveness.

The interviewer has the tough job of finding the right person, a resource, who will meet the challenges and needs of the company. Therefore, it is up to you to help manage the interview in such a way that your very best capabilities are displayed for the interviewer's consideration. You don't want to come off sounding like a "job beggar," but a resource person. And to accomplish that, you have to go in prepared.

Prepare, Prepare, Prepare

Corporate recruiters maintain their "single biggest turn-off" is an applicant's ignorance of the company. "Come prepared with at least five questions for the recruiter [interviewer]," they advise. Sometimes these questions can stand alone; other times they will, in effect, "piggyback" on something the interviewer has said. It doesn't hurt to approach the interview with a high level of curiosity. (Caution: Make sure you don't come across sounding as if you are interrogating the interviewer.)

Your questions should be geared to learning what you need to know about the company—things your research didn't reveal. Because of what you found out in your research, and what you are learning by asking appropriate questions, you can dip into your repertoire of skills and attributes and discuss what is relevant. When you ask questions, be sure you listen attentively so that you come across as a good listener. This is an interpersonal skill very highly valued by employers.

Howard Figler says in *The Complete Job-Search Handbook*:

> The job interview is not a courtroom, where lawyers fight over the right and wrong of what you are saying. The interviewer is not your adversary. He/she is on your side. Interviewers want you to succeed, do well in the interview, because it makes their job easier. . . . Fundamentally, they hope you are the best candidate for the job, because if you are, their job is completed.[5]

The director of placement at the University of Missouri, St. Louis, tells of interviewing a college senior applying for a job at a bank. The student had spent the summer working at another bank, so he was asked about the experience.

"How big is that bank?" he was asked.

"Oh, about three floors," the student said.

End of interview.

The story points out the biggest mistake new graduates make when heading into job interviews: they don't prepare. These days one must prepare, prepare, prepare. The placement director's job was to help students find jobs. She advises that to impress a recruiter, a student should begin in the library studying the company and its industry. The importance of preparation, not just for students but for anyone interviewing for a position, cannot be emphasized strongly enough in today's employment climate. The student or graduate applying for a position has to understand that he or she is competing against legions of seasoned laid-off workers willing to settle even for entry-level jobs.

I was told in letters received from human resource managers and in phone conversations that never in their years of experience have they seen so many applicants for one position. "Just incredible, just incredible," more than one of them said. It was not at all unusual to hear or read, "We have more than five hundred resumes in response to our ad." One San Jose company told me they had received more than fifteen hundred resumes in response to a single ad. I suspect that many ads received more responses than that.

My friend Eddie, who had moved from a top managerial position into an assistant position in human resources just to hang on to a job and a paycheck, told me that on average they were receiving three-inch-high stacks of unsolicited resumes weekly. "We haven't advertised for job openings," she emphasized. "These were all *unsolicited* resumes."

The competition is fierce, underscoring the need to go into an interview well prepared. How do you do that? Here are some pointers:

Fine-tune your common senses or, as Lee Iacocca calls it, savvy or street smarts. This means you are going to need to know something about the company. This will require research at the library (see appendix C). If there is a prominent executive in that company and you know his name, his background may appear in *Who's Who*.

You could also do a trial run at the company. Walk into the lobby, pick up a job description if one is available, gather up any brochures or printed material (a company newsletter), current stock quotation, growth record, recent sales, profits—whatever acquaints you with what is going on there. The more you know, the better leveraged you will be, because you will come across as being informed.

I did this at one corporate headquarters, driving quite a distance, in fact, but it paid off. When I asked for literature about the company, I was told there was none. Later, when I went for the meeting with the human resource manager, I told her what I'd done and expressed surprise. "It occurs to me that quite possibly you really need someone like myself. Writing brochures and literature is one of my fortes," I said.

She smiled at me and replied, "You're very perceptive. You've hit the nail on the head. That's why I invited you in for the interview. Our literature is outdated. I pulled it recently from the table in the lobby. Our growth has been so spectacular that we aren't able to keep up with producing brochures."

This corporation had not advertised for someone like me. It was simply one of the companies I had targeted as a result of my research, and I had sent them a "broadcast letter." I knew it was the third largest company in its field; I knew what its posted earnings had been for the last year; and I knew from an interview I had read in the business section of the paper that it expected to move into second place.

All this and more was in my store of knowledge because I went in prepared. That human resource manager and I became friends. I went to see her twice, and we are still in touch. We developed good chemistry between us. "We need you," she told me, "and I have made the recommendation that they bring you in for an interview, but they aren't prepared to create the position yet." I was asked to maintain communication with them.

Reread the ad to which you applied (if this was an advertised position). After sending out hundreds of resumes, the likelihood is strong that you may not even remember a particular company's ad. (Hopefully, you have kept a good file and record of where you have applied. Ask yourself: What specific qualifications are they looking for? How can I meet those qualifications? How do my qualifications, background, and experience align with the requirements of this position? Make a list of questions you think might be asked, and prepare your answers.

Key Questions You May Be Asked

As to the kind of questions you can expect in an interview, Richard Bolles points out that the questions primarily concern four things:

1. Why are you here?
2. What can you do for us?
3. What kind of person are you?
4. Can we afford you?

Having some idea of what you are going to be asked will help you in making your "sales pitch." Actually, behind every question is another "Why should we hire you?" The interviewer has a mental checklist of what he or she is looking for; it's up to you to demonstrate that *you* are that person.

Typically, an interviewer may begin by asking, "Do you have any questions?" (This approach is used by "behavioral" interviewers who want to avoid canned responses by getting you to take the initiative at the very beginning of the interview.) On several occasions my interviews opened like this, and by asking the right questions, I was provided with the information I needed to fill the gaps in my thinking. Because I was genuinely interested in learning what I needed to know about the company, and showed this, I came across as an astute person.

This is what could be called "a hidden sales opportunity," and research definitely pays off. You will come off sounding up-to-date and informed if you have done your homework. When possible, incorporate an example of your own experience into your questions. Never ask about benefits, salaries, or personnel policies. That would only show greed, not how knowledgeable and achievement-oriented you are. Showcase your knowledge and interest about the firm.

You may run into some tough questions. Knowing your own strengths and weaknesses as they relate to the position should enable you to think in advance about how you could turn any negatives into positives. With good preparation, you will likely increase your ability to approach the interview with more confidence and sensitivity to the most relevant issues that will probably be discussed. Preparation allows you to go in calmer and more organized so that you come off sounding better during the actual interview.

Review your research several times before you go in for the interview. You may want to jot down key points on a three-by-five card, take it with you, and review it before the interview begins. I also found I came across better when I was conversant with current events. I made it a point to watch for relevant tidbits that reflected on a company's type of business. Any company worth its salt would be impressed with someone who showed he or she was "well-rounded." (Caution: Don't tip your hat about your political preference or veer off into discussing controversial subjects.) Remember that preparation builds confidence, and confidence assures excellence under pressure.

The following are some questions that I found were generally asked.

What is your experience? Tell me about yourself. What have you done that will be useful here? The interviewer is not asking for your life history. Choose your answers carefully, keeping in mind that the interviewer is most interested in knowing how you will benefit the company. *Briefly* provide information on your background, always relating what you say to the position for which you are applying. You might ask, "Do you have my resume there?" if you aren't certain he or she does. If so, then you don't have to rehash everything that's on it. Summarize succinctly. This is the time to provide more "bullet" information, the kinds of things you pointed out in your cover letter that weren't on the resume.

You don't want to monopolize the conversation, so don't speak longer than two minutes at a time if you can possibly help it. Include a sentence that will make you memorable.

What are your greatest strengths and weaknesses? With a question like this, it is important to respond so that the "weakness" actually comes across as a strength. For instance, you might say you become a bit impatient when people don't make deadlines. You might say, "I'm a guardian of my time; it's such a valuable commodity. I don't like it when people impinge upon my time and I'm trying to maximize it."

Back any assertions with concrete examples from your work experiences or schooling. The interviewer wants a focus that will show her your high energy level, enthusiasm, assertiveness, decisiveness, social sensitivity, results, or tough-mindedness. She wants you to demonstrate with a brief story (whatever you can provide in two minutes or less) from your background.

Questions often come in two parts. The interviewer may be testing your retention. She may be seeking to determine whether you can answer a two-part question without asking her to repeat the second part. Don't let this trip you up; it's a pretty basic interviewing technique.

What do you know about our company? How do you think your skills will fit in and help us? The interviewer is probing to see if you researched the company. In a survey of 320 company recruiters, a Northwestern University placement director found that "lack of knowledge about the company and industry" ranked with "arrogance/cockiness" and "poor oral communication" as principal job interview turnoffs. "Failure to prepare tells me the person lacks discipline and doesn't care," said one human resource director.

How would you describe yourself? What are your most significant accomplishments? One of the things human resource managers want to know is how you relate to other people. What are your people skills? They won't ask you that directly, but they are trying to make a determination as to how friendly you are and what your interpersonal skills are.

Remember to sell your benefits—your integrity, loyalty, attention to detail, and so on. Provide short examples, experiences that would point out these qualities. (Don't just name them.) "I'm bottom-line conscious," you could say, and back it up with an illustration.

Go in prepared to amplify on at least one outstanding achievement. You might point to your successes in fundraising or a technical skill. "As a result of my efforts at XYZ Corporation, revenues increased from $1.5 million to more than $2 million in just six months. This was accomplished through the recruitment of a small and highly efficient staff whom I trained in sixty days."

What are your career goals? Where do you see yourself in the future? I was asked in an interview with a Fortune 100 company where I would like to be five years from today. I had no hesitation in responding: "I'd like to be right here having proved my worth to the company . . ." (I expanded on that, identifying things that my research had revealed the company was doing and its projections for the future.) You may be asked what your short-range and long-range goals are.

The gentleman interviewing me that day pointed to two huge stacks of resumes and said, "Yours kept rising to the top." He was the second person with whom I interviewed that day. I had gone through an employment agency on this one and was told this company narrowed it down to one other person and myself.

Why are you in the job market? Did you leave your last job? Were you terminated? You must go into your interview prepared to answer that question if it arises. The interviewer will be alert for deceptions, so be direct and quick. "Longer than a minute, and you're dead," cautions one recruiter. Rehearse in your mind just how you will respond in a positive yet truthful manner. If you are out of a job because of downsizing, a merger, or an acquisition, then it is relatively simple to explain. If you are unclear about what happened, you are not alone. Many unemployed people find themselves in that situation.

Even if you were fired, "Your best answer is always the honest one," notes a senior vice president. "With so much corporate budget cutting, being let go doesn't carry the stigma it used to. There's also much more tolerance of job hopping—once a no-no."

Here are some of the reasons Dubin and Keveles list for why people are fired:

- *Style differences.* A new manager comes on board with a different management style.
- *Team play.* Your agenda was perceived as incongruent with the team agenda.
- *Politics.* You didn't go through necessary channels and inadvertently stepped on someone's toes.
- *New team.* The manager wants to create his own team and bring in his own people to establish control.
- *Code of ethics.* Your behavior was incongruent with the company's code of ethics.

- *Contribution level.* Your performance deteriorated, and you were perceived as not being productive enough.
- *Bad fit.* Your particular skills and strengths are no longer seen as a good fit with departmental needs.
- *New goals.* The company has shifted direction and priorities, and the changing emphasis has rendered your job less important or obsolete.
- *Promotion.* You were promoted and then perceived as unable to handle the level of responsibility.
- *Communication style.* Your communication style is unacceptable to those in control.
- *Job elimination.* Your position either is being eliminated or divided up and given to others.
- *Corporate culture.* You may have different values than those of the culture within which you find yourself.[6]

If you were able to accomplish good things on this job even though you were terminated, point to the positive feedback and good performance appraisals you did have. Explain that you were a highly productive, contributing employee, and whatever happened to bring about your dismissal, you are viewing it as a stepping-stone to better things.

Develop in your mind a "separation statement" and then stick to it. Make it concise, one that reflects the truth as you see it and that projects you in a positive light. It is generally wise to write your former employer and/or call the person who was your immediate superior and read him your separation statement, asking for his cooperation so that it won't be difficult for you to get another job.

Protect yourself. Dialogue with your previous employer (or the human resource department, or whomever would be called if a check were to be made on you). In connecting with former managers or colleagues, it is not inappropriate to remind them of your major accomplishments, so refresh their memories, and then thank them in advance for what you feel they will do to help you become reemployed.

As a follow-up to a reference to your previous employment, the interviewer may ask, "What assurance do we have that you would stay with us for any longer than two or three years? I notice that you have skipped around somewhat." He is relating a legitimate concern.

Be honest without coming across as being too defensive. In my own situation I responded by stating that I would like to be very candid and hoped he would appreciate my desire to be honest. Of course the interviewer agreed. I was then able to explain that at the toy company 45 percent of the workforce was terminated, including our department of 150 people; at another place, 36 of us lost our jobs in one day, and a few months later the company was defunct. "I have the letters here from the companies to substantiate this," I said, pointing to my briefcase. (When I left the interview, I left behind copies of those letters.)

I was also able to explain my termination from my last position (about which he shook his head, stating he couldn't understand people like that). I was brief, paying my former employer a compliment as I mentioned his drive and success. Then I stated that he was also known for his impulsiveness and failure to listen to his department manager, who, realizing our employer didn't know all the facts, had strongly advised against my termination. When I finished I asked, "Are there any questions you would like to ask me about this? I'll be happy to answer them."

If you're questioned about your employment history, you might say something like this: "I can understand why you brought that up. If I were in your position, I'd probably ask the same question. Of course you want someone who is loyal, stable, and interested in being with you for the long term . . . ," and then be prepared to provide an answer.

Your strategy should be to redirect the interviewer's thinking to focus on the positives. I explained that my different jobs had given me experience and valuable knowledge and insight that I would be bringing with me into a new position. Be strong in your statements and show determination. You will need to develop your own strategy should this question be posed to you, but very positively seek to convince the interviewer that you regard this new position as a capstone of your career.

What salary are you looking for? Handle this with care. At this stage in the interview process, show yourself to be open to negotiation. *Flexible* is a word commonly used. You can answer, "Flexible within a range," and then ask, "What is your range?" People are accustomed to thinking in terms of ranges. Perks and benefits can make a big difference. Your goal should be to defer specific conversation about compensation until potential employers have had an opportunity to gain a clear sense of your worth and what you can do for them.

The exception to this strategy is when you are talking to a recruiter or career counselor. It's best to be very direct with them, and it won't hurt your chances of getting a job. They need to know what to go after for you and/or how to help you position yourself. Again, you can explain that you are flexible within a range, according to the benefits package and/or other considerations (moving expenses, stock options, car allowance, etc.).

Illegal Questions and How to Handle Them

Companies are pretty savvy these days, but you may run into an interviewer who, in his or her probing, asks some improper questions. This would include: How old are you? Are you married? Are you divorced? Do you plan to have more children? The best defense is no offense—that is, don't get defiant and bristle. If you don't want to answer, just say that you feel the question is irrelevant to your ability to perform the job. Take control and turn the interview back on course. Pull one of your own prepared research questions out of your head and launch it into the air.

Questions actually don't become illegal unless and until it can be proved that they were used against you to screen you out of getting the job. That would be difficult to do, and pursuing this matter costs money. If you are suddenly unemployed, you have to be careful about how you spend your resources. I recommend that you get on with the job hunt.

Make a Good First Impression

Research shows that within the first few seconds of meeting new people, immediate impressions are formed. We do that by sizing others up—their dress, grooming, mannerisms, body language, and speech. We walk into an interview with a credibility gap, and our aim should be to close it as soon as possible by projecting confidence and friendliness.

It's true that sometimes first impressions can be wrong and very deceiving, and once you really get to know a person, you may alter some of your initial perceptions. But in the job interview, it's now or never. Here's what to do.

1. *Walk into the office with assurance and a smile on your face.* Be sure you have the correct pronunciation of the interviewer's name in mind. (Ask the secretary or receptionist if there is any doubt about the pronunciation.) Extend your hand for a firm but gentle handshake and establish direct eye contact. Introduce yourself, pronouncing your name slowly and carefully if the interviewer hasn't done that.

2. *Avoid fidgeting by keeping pens and coffee cups out of your hands.* Drop your hands into your lap and avoid the temptation to use them too much with gestures that, according to the person's understanding of body language, might be misconstrued.

3. *Express admiration about the company*—something you have gleaned from your research, not just the decor or physical plant. (Anybody can do that, and probably the half dozen or more people he or she has interviewed so far have made such comments. Be more creative.) Remember, however, to compliment the company, not the individual. This is called a third party, action-oriented compliment. It is one in which you do not make a judgment yourself but simply report the judgment of someone else. If you are able, and your research has provided you with information, you could pass on some favorable comments that you have heard or read in a news article or industry report.

This shouldn't be just idle flattery or an expression of your opinions. Be real. It will show that you have done some homework. An expression of honest admiration or appreciation requires some effort on your part.

4. *Be conservative in your dress and grooming*—neat, clean, and understated. Look professional. You are selling your professionalism—not your innovative fashion sense. This doesn't mean you have to look like "a corporate clone," but make certain your clothing is suitable for the job for which you are applying. Dress comfortably so that you aren't tugging or adjusting. Avoid looking gaudy, overdressed, or like someone from the distant past. Carry a good attaché or briefcase.

The interviewer is thinking to himself or herself, *What kind of person is this?* Everything you say and do and the way you look will answer that question for him or her. Both intangibles and tangibles will be used in this assessment. This prospective employer must determine whether you will "fit in" with what is going on and the people already employed in the organization.

Before leaving for the interview, stand in front of a full-length mirror and double-check yourself. Is your clothing well-fitted and pressed? Are your shoes polished? Nothing spoils your appearance more than scuffed, run-down-at-the-heels shoes. Are your fingernails nicely manicured? Are your makeup and hairstyle conservative? Avoid huge hoop earrings and clunky jewelry. Keep it simple.

A midwestern manufacturing company advertised for an industrial sales position. Here's how the president of the company summarized the experience of the interviewing process:

> We received more resumes than we expected. We needed some way to prequalify the applicants, because, based on experience, most of them wouldn't pass muster anyway.
>
> We decided that since that position was in sales, we wanted someone who could sell himself or herself. Because the job involves both written (correspondence) and personal sales, we disregarded any resume that didn't have a cover letter written specifically in response to our ad. . . .
>
> As for the interview, the best advice is the most difficult to follow, unless one is experienced at interviewing. Be natural. Any forced mannerisms, speech patterns and expressions come through very quickly. Younger people may feel nervous, but experienced interviewers usually are able to factor it out of their evaluation.
>
> Answer questions as thoroughly as possible in the fewest words possible. That means no extra, unnecessary words. Think about this. It is important. One application was pretty good on all other points, but, boy, did he ramble. We want someone to answer customers' questions, not put them to sleep, as almost happened to me. . . .
>
> Oh, one more point. Don't lie about your jobs. Even one lie or unexplained lapse of time that a reference check uncovered could cost you a shot at the job. . . .
>
> A series of interviews is like getting picked up and slammed down—again and again. There's no one, set formula of which I'm aware that will guarantee success.
>
> Following the suggestions here may, at best, save time, energy, and money, and possibly even lessen some frustration that can be so defeating.[7]

Ten Basic Attitudes and Techniques for Putting Yourself Across Correctly in an Interview

1. Sell yourself.
2. Link yourself and your background to the job.
3. Emphasize specific accomplishments.
4. Always maintain a professional posture and tone.
5. Pick up cues from your interviewer.
6. Believe in your own myths: being the ideal candidate means acting and thinking about yourself as you are at your best.
7. Don't apologize: Interviewing apologetically is a common mistake, made most often by people who feel they're too young, too old, or over- or underqualified for the job they are seeking—which covers just about everyone.
8. Never say "Maybe." Always sound positive during the interview.
9. Summarize your main points periodically. A good trick to sounding professional is to number your accomplishments: "There are three major reasons why I feel this job is right for me. One . . ." Statements like this make you sound organized and intelligent. This advice is frequently given by career, media, and political consultants.
10. Close the interview. "I'm looking forward to talking with you further about this job; as I've said, I'm very enthusiastic about it and know I could make a significant contribution to your company . . ." [words to this effect]. Be yourself.[8]

After the Interview

"What do you do after the interview besides chastise yourself with 'If onlys'?" an unemployed acquaintance asked.

207

Robert Half, president of Robert Half International, Inc., says we're all amateurs at job interviews. Analyze what went wrong. Work on the assumption that something *did.* "If you can honestly figure out your mistakes, you won't make them again at the next interview."

But forget the "If onlys," I told my acquaintance. "You went in prepared, didn't you?" He assured me he had. "Commit it to God in prayer and get on with your life," I told him. "Chastising yourself is enervating. Who needs it? We learn from our mistakes, but we don't have to beat ourselves over the head with them."

No matter how you feel you did, the job interview doesn't end at the smile-and-handshake stage. Immediately write a note thanking the interviewer for his or her time. List one or more reasons and briefly summarize why you feel you are right for the position, but don't rehash everything that was discussed during the appointment.

If you have come across something—an article from a newspaper or trade journal—that pertains to what was discussed during the interview, include it. If appropriate, send a work sample that relates to specific skills the interviewer said he or she was looking for. If there were unanswered questions—something the interviewer asked for and you needed to look up—include that information with your letter.

This kind of follow-up is very wise. Not everyone does this, and it's just one more way for you to stand head and shoulders above the pack. Have someone proofread your letter before you send it. It's easy for typos or errors to slip in.

If you haven't heard from the company at the end of two weeks, call and ask if a decision has been reached. Express your ongoing interest in the position. More than likely you will not be able to reach the person with whom you interviewed, but there is no harm in trying. Kindly request that he or she be notified that you did call and are still interested.

You can do it! Here's a prayer you can pray before you go in for that all-important interview:

Dear God, give me wisdom, insight, and discernment. Help me to keep my mouth shut when it should be shut, to ask appropriate questions when it should be open, and to answer questions intelligently when I'm asked. Quiet my fears. Help me to project what you would have me project. May I find favor in this interview. Amen.

Wisdom is a divine endowment and not a human acquisition. "If any of you lacks wisdom, he should ask God, who gives generously to all without finding fault, and it will be given to him" (James 1:5 NIV).

13

The Job Offer

It has been said that recognition may be the workplace's single most sought-after reward, but good compensation comes in a strong second.

If you have done a good job, your resumes, cover letters, networking, and research have earned you interviews with hiring authorities. Your hard work has paid off, and you have landed a job offer. Of all the facets of looking for the right position, the art of negotiating requires the greatest measure of discipline, preparation, and confidence on your part.

Dick Lathrop says, "There may be others who applied there who could have done the job better than you. But it is true today, and it will ever be true. The person who gets hired is not necessarily the one who can do that job best, but the one who knows the most about how to get hired."

At this point you may be so weary of the job search and so desperate financially, that you are ready to jump at anything. You may be thinking, *How can I possibly negotiate on this offer? I need it so badly!* But what do you have to lose by negotiation? The most you have to lose is that the employer will stand firm on his offer. It is very unlikely that he will withdraw it. If push comes to shove, go for the offer as it stands. Don't sabotage what could turn into something great down the line.

Assessing the Offer

Some basic principles of negotiation should be taken into consideration and can be applied regardless of the employment climate. First, it doesn't hurt, and in fact isn't very savvy, not to aim for the best in the negotiation process. Just bear in mind that dozens of people are waiting in line, competing for the same job you are being offered. State up front that you are flexible and willing to negotiate, and be sure the person making the job offer understands that and hears you correctly.

Second, as you assess the offer, understand that there are no job utopias. In any event, hold your head erect, maintain your dignity, and always remember that God is the one in control of your destiny. Money follows value, and obviously you are considered a person of value. Your interviewing performance proved that and got you where you are now.

I was told by a career counselor that few people realize it, but the most important thing you can negotiate is not a dollar figure. Far more important is the nature of the job itself. Once the responsibility and budget associated with a job have been determined, a given salary range will be indicated. Your research should have already established for you what the compensation in your field is and your place in it. Of course you don't want to sell yourself short; on the other hand, you shouldn't attempt to drive such a hard bargain that the employer would feel you have held his feet to the fire. Don't haggle. Instead, focus on mutual gains and obtain what you are entitled to as an outcome of an open, fair, and intelligent dialogue. As the Bible says, "A workman is worthy of his wages" (Luke 10:7).

Finally, in assessing the position, one area open for negotiation is the level of responsibility. It should be commensurate with the compensation, and you should know what your work is able to command in the marketplace so that if it becomes necessary, you can point this out and provide examples.

Using the Internet to Advantage

The U.S. Department of Labor Bureau of Labor Statistics site at www.bls.gov provides more information than you will know what to do with! You will find wages by area and occupation, earnings by industry, employee benefits, employment costs, state and county wages for a given locale, national compensation rates, and more.

The Occupational Outlook Handbook also provides ballpark figures for a select list of jobs and can be accessed on the Internet at www.bls.gov also. If salary information on your particular position isn't found, you may want to ask a reference librarian at your library to help you find salary information.

Salary Considerations

Another place to determine what salary ranges are in a given locale is to learn the name of an association or professional group for the position in which you are interested and consult the *Encyclopedia of Associations*, volume 1, at the library. You can also use your network to identify pay scales for the job you have targeted.

If you are being asked to relocate, say from the Midwest to California, you will need to take into consideration the higher housing and transportation costs. A change in your salary may be necessary if you are hoping to replicate your standard of living in a new locale. Cost-of-living differences in a new location and mortgage differentials should be factored into your assessment of a job offer. The more you know about what kind of money you can command, the better prepared you are to prove yourself a smart, skilled veteran of the work world. When you know what the top wage is in your field and how to ask for it, you not only may win the best possible paycheck but also will enhance your employer's perception of your value. Demonstrate what you're worth, and the possibility exists that you are halfway there in winning it.

Ask for a reasonable length of time to assess any offer. That's expected. Employers understand that a person needs time. Try to resist the temptation to accept an offer on the spot. Of course, if the offer looks good, is what you really want, and is within the range of what you know you are worth in today's job market, then accept it. But if certain aspects of the job don't meet your expectations and criteria, then seek to negotiate a better package.

How can you do that and maintain a competitive edge? You could tell your prospective employer, "I really appreciate this offer and am delighted that you see me as a good fit within your organization. I know I can make a major contribution to your goals, but I would like a little time to give this careful thought."

Give yourself a day or two or more, depending on what else you might have going for you. Buy yourself some time, investigate, and learn more. Make some calls if you have other prospects, and let those employers know you have an offer. Ask where you stand with them. Assessing a job offer really narrows down to three components: (1) the position itself, (2) the company, and (3) the salary and benefits package.

Pay negotiation is a crucial skill. Columnist Joyce Lain Kennedy points out that you can always lower your price, but it is a straight-up rock climb to get it raised after you have accepted a job offer. She advises that you come at it like this:

> The next time you hear the low-pay pitch, say nothing. Smile, look at the floor and wait until a dollar amount is named. If it's under the market rate, be slow to answer, wipe the smile off your face and keep looking at the floor. Sometimes an improved offer fills the uncomfortable silence. If not, hold off as long as you can, then begin with a restatement of your key assets and confidently say that one of the reasons they would be hiring you is to improve the profit picture and that you're thinking of a range between $X and $Y.
>
> If pushed to talk dollar figures first, collect yourself for five or six seconds and use the same no-hesitation strategy just described. You can add, "Considering that you want the best person you can find for this position in these difficult times, I think that's both market rate and fair, don't you agree?"[1]

Kennedy's advice is wise and practical. She underscores that pay dickering is a learnable skill that you will need often in the years ahead as job tenure shortens and globalization wrecks the best of career plans. There are many books that will enhance your learning about pay negotiation. Kennedy suggests these: Herb Cohen's *You Can Negotiate Anything*; Jack Chapman's *Negotiating Your Salary: How to Make $1,000 a Minute*; and Daniel Porot and Francis B. Haynes's *101 Salary Secrets: How to Negotiate Like a Pro*.

The Position: Matching the Passions in Your Heart with the Job

A well-intentioned friend, seeking to offer encouragement and commiserate with me, wrote: "As a friend, could I throw one observation your way as you seek your next job? It seemed almost from the time you took the position at ___'s place that you were unhappy and realized you were not in the right place. To what extent did this affect your performance? I would encourage you to look for a situation that matches the passions God has planted in your heart. I'll be praying for you."

At first reading I was hurt. Then a little anger crept in. To my husband I complained, "He's calling into question my job performance." I defended myself, pointing out how hard I'd worked, the good things that had been accomplished, how I'd gone the second mile.

Then reason took over. My friend's words had made an impact. It didn't happen immediately, and I was forced to live with what was going on in my head and heart for several days.

Finally it dawned on me. Ever since accepting that particular position I'd had to explain why I was where I was. I hadn't sought the job, but it came right at the time when we were feeling the need to make a change. My husband's health required that he take a sabbatical, and the need for that had made itself known on several occasions.

I don't know what your circumstances are. If you have been unemployed for any length of time at all, they are probably quite pressing and you are feeling a sense of neediness. Such neediness can force us into uncomfortable positions where we are compelled to make difficult choices that don't always measure up to our expectations. We may, for instance, have to make a major move out of state. Such was our case. We didn't have small children or teenagers to uproot from school and friends, so that was not a complicating factor, but it may be for you.

From the outset, the place where I worked made me uncomfortable. My friend's assessment was correct. The work itself was not a problem and, in fact, as my husband and I weighed the pluses and the minuses (a good idea, simple to do—two columns on a sheet of paper is all it takes), the pluses outweighed the minuses. After prayerful consideration, we made the move. Still, I found myself making explanations.

"C. S. Lewis wrote that he came kicking and screaming into the kingdom of God," I'd say, responding to questions from friends about the work, "and that's how I came to this job." Seeking to get others to understand the embarrassment and discomfiture I was experiencing forced me to offer an explanation. "Bruce was right," I finally admitted to my husband. "It was a bad fit from day one."

I highlight this to underscore in your thinking the importance of trying to match the passions in your heart to the right job. If you are forced to make a decision that runs counter to your belief system or to some of the criteria you have established that you would like to see fulfilled in this next job, stop and think. What will the trade-offs be? In order to get that paycheck, what compromises are you going to have to make?

Ask yourself, "Do I mesh with the people with whom I will be working and associating as a whole?" That's not easy to assess, but if you have rapport with the top-level people with whom you have interviewed, that would be a positive indicator.

Be sure you ask for and receive a written job description. This will be very helpful as you assess the position. It is also a good delaying tactic, enabling you to sleep on the offer a few nights more. You will eventually want to ask for the offer in a letter, but only after you have done some initial negotiating.

If possible, you might try to find out what happened to the person who preceded you in this prospective position. What is the average tenure of positions in this organization? And how does this position fit in with your short- and long-range career plans?

Reviewing the Job Offer in Light of God's Will

Another issue that must be raised as you assess the job offer is to what extent you have involved God in your job search. Nothing happens to us that doesn't first filter through God's hands. The will of God will never take you where the grace of God cannot keep you. My husband and I experienced this. At some point a sense of peace should settle upon you—the knowledge that God is in this with you and will provide strength and resources to enable you to do what has to be done.

In seeking God's will about a job offer, we must always reckon with the possibility that there are times when God asks us to make difficult choices. Other doors simply may not have opened, and you are at brink's edge. Choices and options are not in plentiful supply. God knows your need, and this position has become available. You have prayed; friends and family have prayed. You have done all the right things; no stones have been left unturned. You have earnestly implored God to come to your rescue. The heavens seem as brass. And now this: a job offer.

But suppose the offer doesn't quite meet all your expectations. Indeed, the passion in your heart doesn't quite match the job. What are you supposed to do? First Peter 4:19 says, "Trust yourself to the God who made you, for he will never fail you" (TLB).

The Bible is God's Word to you. It is unfailing in providing wisdom and hope. Our heavenly Father takes no pleasure in seeing his children dissatisfied with that which consumes eight or more hours of their day. Ecclesiastes 5:18 makes it clear that it is "good and fitting . . . to enjoy oneself in all one's labor in which he toils under the sun during the few years of his life which God has given him" (NASB). The truth is that the average person spends over 97,760 hours at work in a lifetime. Shouldn't you make the most of it?

God may be leading you into strange and unaccustomed paths, but you can have the assurance that he will go before you to prepare the way. As you move ahead, one step at a time, trusting him, he will do for you what you cannot do for yourself. Psalm 37:5 says, "Commit your way to the LORD, trust also in Him, and He shall bring it to pass."

Moreover, when you dip your feet into the river, as it were, and the water parts and you move on, even then, if you have "heard" him wrong or have acted impulsively or hastily, God can be trusted to make all things work together for your good. That's Romans 8:28 in action. Sometimes we may honestly believe that we have done the right thing, but time and circumstances show us that we have put our feet into the wrong river. The net gain, however, can be one of joy, knowing that what we did was done in loving obedience to what we felt was the prompting of God's own Holy Spirit.

Plans are good; they allow God to work in the personal chaos that has disrupted our lives. And if we have gone in the wrong direction, God can be trusted to get through to us and turn us in another way. This calls for flexibility and tenacity, which we need as much during the time we are evaluating a job offer as we did while we were job hunting.

God can order our stops as well as our steps. He has even been known to throw roadblocks in our way that were so obvious we knew we had to stop, turn around, and go back to where we were in our thinking processes. If we trip, fall, get his signals wrong, or make a mistake in judgment, it's not the end of the world. God can be counted on to see us through. In the process, we will learn some lessons we might never otherwise have learned. If I sound like I am speaking from experience, you've got that right! Don't give up on yourself. And never give up on God.

Sometimes what we view as a mistake is actually God's plan for instructing us. He isn't out to get us or punish us, although we don't always understand what is happening at the time. Did you understand everything your parents were doing when they imposed some restraints on you as a child or teenager? When they asked difficult things of you, did you sometimes have cause to wonder? Just so, the Bible tells us, we don't always understand God's parenting of us. But he always has our best interests at heart.

Remember that God has plans for you, to give you a future and hope (see Jer. 29:11). Joy does not have to be a "ha-ha" kind of thing. Happiness is a choice, and it isn't dependent on the quality of our circumstances. God will empower us to rise above our emotional state if we involve him in our plans and apply biblical principles in our decision making. Psalm 37:23–24 says, "The steps of a good man are ordered by the LORD, and He delights in his way. Though he fall, he shall not be utterly cast down; for the LORD upholds him with His hand." In ever so many ways the Bible informs us that God will instruct us and teach us the way we should go. He promises to guide us in the process (see Ps. 32:8).

Keep these things in mind as you weigh the job offer. It may not be a job utopia, but it will no doubt present unique challenges. Obviously you can handle these challenges or you wouldn't have been selected for the position. You have edged out many others and are highly regarded by this prospective employer. He or she is staking a lot on you.

I developed a philosophy while working on the job that didn't quite match all the passions in my heart. I called it "TP." When things happened that were an embarrassment and I wanted to run and hide, or when I was distressed over the treatment of co-workers or other people, I would say to myself: "TP. TP." Translated that means, "Think paycheck!" I wasn't being mercenary. All of us need a means to make a living unless we have a rich benefactor who puts us in his or her will and enables us to live on "Easy Street" for the rest of our lives.

At that job I learned to do something else that helped enormously as well. I would close my office door, spread out my hands palms up, lift my arms slowly into the air, and say, "I release it, Lord. It's in your hands." Just doing that brought a sense of peace, and I could get on with what had to be done.

In any job we can learn coping skills. As you assess this position, evaluate the self-esteem factor, the contribution this job might make to the lives of others, and whatever other factors are important to you. You just might be surprised at what will develop as a result of taking the position. A guiding principle in my life has always been to do whatever I had to do as unto the Lord, and not just unto men (or my employer). God himself is a rewarder, and not all the rewards are handed out down here. A favorite Bible passage that has seen me through many a challenging time is Colossians 3:23–24: "Whatever you do, do it heartily, as to the Lord and not to men, knowing that from the Lord you will receive the reward of the inheritance; for you serve the Lord Christ."

Certainly my husband and I had no way of knowing that the dearest friends we could ever hope to make would be made in the city where I accepted that difficult position. Granted, we invest a lot of ourselves and our time in our work, but that isn't everything. There is life beyond work. A great tragedy occurs when a person stakes everything on his or her career. Jobs come and go. If you don't have a solid relationship with Christ when the rug is pulled out from under you, you will land hard. But if you are secure in your relationship with the Father through the Son, you will get up and walk on confident in him.

Admittedly, when we are in a work situation that isn't a good fit or that is in violation of our conscience, we are going to be out of sync. At some point it may reflect in our attitude and lead to job loss.

We exhibit our values through our demeanor, as well as through the words we express. An unfulfilling job can frustrate one's dreams and values. When those dreams are put on hold because we need a paycheck to survive, we feel stuck. *How do I get out of this?* we may think. *My back is to the wall. What hope is there for the future?* Going to work is like climbing a personal Mount Everest every day. Change seems unattainable.

At this point we need to rein in our thoughts once again, reminding ourselves that God knows where we are. He hasn't abdicated his position. You have a destiny, and God is going to orchestrate the events in your life to help you attain what is going to happen next.

At one point I had to confess to God that I probably hadn't "heard" him correctly a time or two. I even had to say I may have wanted my own way more than his will. Honest confession. God delights in it. (He sees into our hearts anyway!) And he is wise and loving enough not to let us hang ourselves on our mistakes or wrong judgment.

Assessing the Company

Howard Figler points out, "Most people look for new employment as though they were walking the plank—blindfolded, hands bound, last rites on their lips, hoping everything will work out okay."[2]

Ideally, you checked out the company that has offered you a job, its assets, the people at the top, and so on before you even applied, and your research revealed it to be a sound organization with a good track record. If you didn't do so then, now is the time. In these days of mergers, acquisitions, and takeovers, you need to learn all you can about a company's strengths and weaknesses.

Oftentimes people will say, "If I had known what this job was like before getting into it, I never would have gotten into it!" Foresight is better than hindsight, but I don't know anyone who has a crystal ball to peer into that will caution us. We do have someone to go to, however. We have God.

Over and over again I turned to God's Word for guidance. I always came away refreshed, renewed in spirit, able to go on. My husband and I involved others in praying for and with us. In a multitude of counselors there is wisdom, the wisdom writer says, and we listened to people whose counsel we really valued. We heeded their advice and asked God not to let us make mistakes.

Do your homework, investigate the company, and talk to people who may be in the know. Read the company literature. Playing detective is not out of order as you assess a company. This is your life, your future, your time, your energy. You are investing in you. At some point you may need to moderate your expectations, but that doesn't mean you discard them completely. Just make sure you are being realistic in your evaluation.

Basically, you will need to find out if the company is going someplace. Is it gaining or losing market share? Would you be working in a strong division—a part of the company where your expertise can be challenged and you can show your stuff? If you can't get good answers to those questions, you have to ask yourself a tough question: Will the rewards of this job be worth it? Whether it's a nonprofit organization, a ministry, a government position, a corporate environment, a family-owned enterprise, a small business, or something else, the same questions apply. You will have to get a feel for the company and its niche within the industry.

Another thing your detective work might seek to uncover is the potential for upward mobility. Are you going to be stuck in a position, or will you have opportunity for advancement? If there is no mobility in the nature of the position itself, what about financially? All of us like to feel we are going forward in life. It is good to know you are with a company that is progressive. Don't be too assertive or pushy in your inquiries at the time the job is offered, but do seek to come across as someone who would not be content with the status quo. You want to make a difference and a contribution that will count. You need to know that your efforts will be noticed and compensated accordingly.

Assessing the Salary and Benefits Package

If everything looks good, accept the job. If certain aspects look bad, negotiate for a better package. If all aspects look bad, ask yourself why in the world you interviewed for the job in the first place! (Learn from the experience, and if you can afford to keep up the job search, don't accept the offer. Keep on keeping on until that right job comes along.)

Salaries for a particular job may vary in different parts of the country. A nonprofit organization usually will not pay what a corporation pays for the same kind of work. Negotiation is an interactive process in which you and your prospective employer shape the entire job package. Employers usually expect to negotiate, and the salary for most jobs is flexible within a specific range. To remember this is to allay some of your fears.

Is it possible to underprice yourself and leave a lot of money on the table? Is it possible to overprice yourself and put an abrupt end to the offer? That's the dilemma we face as we confront a job offer. We don't want to be too high in our request, yet we certainly don't want to be too low. How can we be on target?

The answer lies in not only assessing the salary being offered but also in factoring in the fringe benefits as much as possible. This would include as part of a standard package medical, dental, optical, accidental death, life and disability insurance, pension, and vacation and holiday pay. But it doesn't have to be limited to that. The higher up you are on the pay scale, the more corporate perks (properly known as perquisites) there are to take into consideration, such as a contract for a specified number of years with a severance package that would include compensation in case of merger, outplacement marketing and relocation assistance in the event of termination, a six-month extension of all insurance benefits after leaving, a company car, travel expenses, a company credit card, annual renegotiation upward, stock options, and profit sharing.

There are many forms of compensation other than base salary. These vary by industry and occupational specialty and with the economic environment. Consider these options that greatly increase the value of a compensation package: performance bonuses; productivity-based incentive increases; flex plans (the employee designs his or her own package of benefits from a variety of options); counseling services; tax, financial, and legal advice; educational benefits; dependent scholarships; child care assistance; moving, in-transit, and relocation assistance; performance reviews and opportunities for promotion; membership in health clubs and leisure facilities; discounts or business reimbursements for travel; professional association fees; and publication incentives.

You may think of other fringe benefits unique to your situation that you would like to see included in your compensation package. While money is certainly an important issue, so is the opportunity for advancement and the prospect of long-term employment. We tend to think the job that pays the most is necessarily the best. For several reasons, it can be a mistake to simply go for the highest-paying job. Economic gain can come in a variety of ways. Early in a career, for instance, the quality of learning is more important than earnings. Quality learning in lieu of high pay will stand you in good stead and enhance your career market value in years to come.

Starting salaries in certain fields may be low, especially for those with less experience. It's quite common knowledge that advertising, publishing, and banking are relatively low-paying jobs at the outset, but this is, in part, because of a weeding-out process. To put it another way, cream always rises to the top, and those who stay in such jobs and perform well will earn significant salaries before too long.

More is not always better. Think, as stockbrokers do, in terms of *futures*. The quality of a work relationship and its future potential must be taken into consideration. Potential earnings are as important as present earnings if you can manage the present earnings in your particular situation. Sometimes you have to let your earning potential develop.

Beware that you do not get caught in stereotypes about the earning potential in a given field. "You can't live on their kind of income" is often heard. Not necessarily so. That's a stereotype. Do some research. Check with people in a specified field. "Can you tell me what the range in salary is in this field?" is a safe question. *Range* is a key word to use.

Three things to bear in mind particularly are: (1) identify pay scales for the job you have targeted; (2) identify pay scales in the appropriate industry for this kind of job; and (3) identify pay scales in a geographic location.

The message is that if you don't ask, you won't get. You will likely have practically no leverage after you have accepted a job offer.

Listed below are certain major items that may be open to some negotiation.

athletic club/fitness center	company car, gas allowance
base salary	company purchase of your home
bonus	consulting fees after termination
child care assistance	consumer product discounts
closing costs	country club membership

CPA and tax assistance
deferred compensation
expense account
financial planning assistance
insurance benefits after termination
in-transit expenses
legal assistance
life insurance
lodging while between homes
matching investment program
medical insurance
mortgage prepayment penalty
other insurance
overseas travel
pension plan

professional outplacement
profit sharing
real estate fees
reimbursement of:
  moving expenses
   mortgage rate differential
sales commission
severance pay
shipping of boats, pets
short-term loan
stock options
trips and expenses while looking for a
   home
vacations

A general rule is that the older and more experienced you are, the more important your benefits are. If you are young, consider the experience and exposure the job will give you well ahead of any benefits package. According to most career specialists with whom I consulted, a good benefits package can be worth 20 to 40 percent of your salary. For more information on benefits, go to the Bureau of Labor Statistics (www.bls.gov).

A Win-Win Process

Negotiating shouldn't hurt your chances with a firm if handled correctly. It can be a win-win process for the employer and you.

Kenneth and Sheryl Dawson suggest these additional basic negotiation tactics to orchestrate a win-win equation:

1. Always negotiate with the hiring authority, not with the human resource department.

2. Let the employer name a salary figure first. (You're flexible.)
3. Never answer the question, "What is the minimum you'll accept?" or "How much money do you need to make?" (You're not interested in minimums.)[3]

The Dawsons suggest you strap on your seat belt and accelerate for a mutually beneficial best deal. Prove that you are not a formidable adversary but that this prospective employer is fortunate to have you as an ally.

Once successful negotiations have taken place and you have accepted the job offer, it is wise to formalize your agreement with a letter of understanding. You will find that some companies automatically do this, while others do not, and you may have to ask for it. You could also provide your own.

Below is a formula for evaluating a job offer. Remember, your next job is what you make of it. Careful consideration now will help you land the job of your dreams.

Formula for Evaluating a Job Offer

Value of a Job Offer = Starting Salary
+ Long-run earning potential
+ Possible secondary gains
+ New learning acquired
+ Quality of co-workers
+ Challenge of the job
+ Lifestyle considerations

14

When You Don't Get
the Job Offer

It's going to happen—if it hasn't already—and when it does, you are going to experience a letdown. At some point you will receive what I call "thanks but no thanks" letters.

I f you have been unemployed for any length of time, you know how those "thanks but no thanks" letters read: "Your qualifications were impressive, but the position was given to someone whose credentials more closely matched what we were looking for."

When you receive letters like that, you experience many of the emotional reactions you had when you first learned that you had lost your job—feelings of rejection, failure, hopelessness. The temptation is always there to succumb to despair, to give up. Isaiah 43:2 speaks of going through water and fire experiences. But it assures us we won't drown nor be burned or scorched. I love the way Warren Wiersbe speaks of this experience: "When God permits his children to go

229

through the furnace, he keeps his eye on the clock and his hand on the thermostat. His loving heart knows how much and how long" (1 Peter 1:6–7, paraphrase by Wiersbe).

I kept Wiersbe's paraphrase within sight during my job search. I found myself turning to favorite Bible passages that had seen me through crisis moments before. Often I retreated to a secluded place with favorite books tucked under my arm. Another encouraging quote came from A. W. Tozer in *The Root of the Righteous*:

> A thousand distractions would woo us away from thoughts of God, but if we are wise we will sternly put them from us and make room for . . . Him. Some things may be neglected with but little loss to the spiritual life, but to neglect communion with God is to hurt ourselves where we cannot afford it. God will respond to our efforts to know Him. The Bible tells us how; it is altogether a matter of how much determination we bring to the holy task.[1]

We need reinforcement and reassurance that we are going to make it. The neglected heart and life will experience chaos. The creeping wilderness will soon take over the person who trusts in his or her own strength and forgets to pray and turn to the Bible. Time after time I said, "I don't see how people make it in this job climate if they aren't turning to God!"

Some people won't understand and will say we are using God as a prop or crutch. They think of him as a disappointment—a heavenly bellhop who hasn't responded to their wishes. They regard him as a perennial grievance, a resident policeman, a God for the elite, or a God of history—for the dead perhaps but not for the living.

J. B. Phillips discusses all of these erroneous impressions and more in his classic *Your God Is Too Small*. Phillips helped me to grasp the concept of God operating with unimpaired energy in the present—my present, your present—that will lead to a hopeful future. "God will inevitably appear to disappoint the man who is attempting to use him as a convenience, a prop, or a comfort, for his own plans. God has never been known to disappoint the man who is sincerely wanting to cooperate with his own purposes."[2]

God is not an absentee potentate. He is not a *little* God. He is not the party leader of a particular point of view. He is more than a magnificent human being; more than an idea. He is, the Bible assures us, "a very present [real] help in trouble" (see Ps. 46:1). That means he is ever-present, mighty, and well-proved. Because of this awesome truth—which is ours to hold on to in *our* times of trouble—we do not have to fear. "The LORD is good, a stronghold [refuge] in the day of trouble; and He knows [cares for] those who trust in Him" (Nah. 1:7).

Keep Yourself Focused

A. W. Tozer says it would be a tragedy indeed to come to the place where we have no other but God and find that we had not really been trusting him. The most important thing I can urge you to do is to keep yourself focused on God. While you may experience disappointment and some letdowns, you will not stay down. "God has a better plan," I would say. "I just have to keep on asking, seeking, knocking, and believing. The right door will open. Jeremiah 29:11 is still in the Bible."

Tozer explains that it would be better to invite God now to remove every false trust, to disengage our hearts from all secret hiding places and bring us out into the open where we can discover for ourselves whether or not we actually trust him. "That is a harsh cure for our troubles," he admits, "but it is a sure one. Gentler cures may be too weak to do the work. And time is running out on us."[3]

To trust when we feel betrayed, afraid, overwhelmed, angry, and treated unfairly is not always easy, we have to

231

admit. But to admit this is not to diminish your faith or to incur God's wrath.

What Happens When You Don't Get the Job Offer?

I remember only too well the emotional high I experienced when I received a phone call from the human resource director at a well-known northern California hospital. She elaborated on what had captured her attention out of the five hundred or more resumes she had received. I had sent a color photocopy of the front cover of a nationally known magazine that portrayed the person in the lead article I had ghosted. *For sure*, I thought, *this will be the job.*

I clearly violated the "rules" by including a color photocopy with my resume. Obviously, a job seeker can't send color photocopies with a thousand resumes or even a hundred. And I readily recognize that not everyone reading this is an author. You may, no doubt, be thinking you don't have that advantage. But that call prompted me to send color photocopies with the next dozen or so resumes. I didn't receive any more phone calls like that, nor did my efforts result in landing a job. Instead, I landed flat on my face, or splattered on the ceiling, as my friend Barb Johnson would say.

And I don't mind telling you—in fact, you need to know—that at times I was disappointed with God. I experienced a lot of anger, and the emotional roller coaster was devastating. I recalled time after time the Bible verses I have referred to in this book. I cried out to God with tears of sadness. "This shouldn't be happening to us, God," I would say. "We are your children. We've been in this 'furnace' a long time."

I tell you this because I want you to understand that what you are experiencing is real. You don't have to be ashamed or apologize. God understands. You owe no one explanations. But you also need to understand this: God has his reason for delays, and he doesn't owe you explanations either.

We can't wish the "Why?" questions away. We are trapped in the present, and we can't see the end from the beginning. I have had to remind myself of this often. Our problem is myopia—a defective vision, a too narrow view, a lack of discernment. That is why I emphasize the need to keep our focus where it belongs—on God himself, trusting beyond the optic nerve, using our eyes of faith. That was what Job had to do in his time of distress. He said to God, "I know that you can do all things; no plan of yours can be thwarted" (Job 42:2 NIV).

Philip Yancey takes the wraps off three questions no one asks aloud, for at best they seem impolite, at worst heretical: Is God unfair? Is he silent? Hidden?

Yancey points to Job, as many writers do who attempt to tackle these questions. He reminds us that unfairness, as we perceive it, is no easier for us to swallow today than it was for Job thousands of years ago.

The tension in our thinking comes about as a result of contemplating the world as it is versus the world as it ought to be. Job loss and the problems it imposes shouldn't happen to good, upright people like you and me. And that's what Job and his friends thought too as they sparred in their verbal boxing match. Job complained, "When I hoped for good, evil came; when I looked for light, then came darkness. The churning inside me never stops" (Job 30:26–27 NIV). "Job's strident message of life's unfairness seems peculiarly suited to our own pain-racked century," Yancey says. What then are we to conclude? Simply that *life on earth is unfair*. Why deny it? Jesus didn't.

But here's what we *must* remember: God responded to life's unfairness not with words, but with a visit. "Jesus offers flesh-and-blood proof of how God feels about unfairness, for he took on the 'stuff' of life. He gave, in summary, a final answer to all lurking questions about the goodness of God," writes Yancey. We all yearn for a "fault-proof" world, but unfairness will not disappear until we have that new heaven and new earth the Bible tells us will happen one day.

It is the cross that reveals for us what kind of world we have. Look at it and remember what people did to the Son of God. Yancey writes, "Jesus offered no immunity, no way *out* of the unfairness, but rather a way *through* to the other side."[4]

Yancey says the Bible offers two cures: *remember the past and consider the future.* God doesn't enjoy keeping his children in the dark. God's answer to Job's accusations of unfairness clearly show that until we know a little more about running the physical universe, we shouldn't attempt to tell God how to run the moral universe (read Job 38–39). Job ended up putting his hand over his mouth (Job 40:4).

Job's churning did stop; yours will too. The day will come when you are once again employed (read Job 42).

15

Final Considerations

God isn't short on ideas. We may feel we are, but he definitely isn't!

While seeking to become reemployed, sometimes we encounter obstacles, a bombardment of negatives. The job market is tough—in some respects probably tougher than it has ever been before.

Erwin Lutzer writes in *Failure: The Back Door to Success*, "At this present moment, our future is more important than our past. We have no claim on the past, but we do have a claim on the future. The past is closed; the future is yet open for new possibilities. But we cannot live a meaningful life in the future if we are tied to the failures or successes of the past."[1]

An unemployed man wrote to a midwestern newspaper saying that if you want proof positive that you are worthless, unworthy of consideration, insignificant, and in fact contemptible, you should conduct a job search. He maintained that if honors existed in the categories of rudeness, insensitivity, tactlessness, and sheer bloody-minded dumb insolence, the walls of his city's business community would be crowded with testimonial plaques.

His summation of the treatment received by the job hunter is fairly accurate in many respects. However, considering the number of unemployed people and the many thousands of resumes, letters, and phone calls businesses receive (many unsolicited), perhaps we should try to be a bit more understanding.

This writer says you can expect to have the phone hung up in your ear, to be treated coldly, and to hear more than a trace of impatience in the voices of the persons you manage to reach. He cautions that you can expect to be dealt with as a nuisance.

He describes their letters as insincere, some inept, some brutal, and a good number simply an insult to the intelligence. He admits that there are some honorable exceptions; that sometimes—not often—he was treated with a measure of respect and consideration. He asked, "What's to be done?" How can we reduce the impact of the hindrances?

I saved addressing these issues for this chapter, because at this juncture, after a prolonged job search, this man's description of what happens may be a fairly accurate portrayal of what you have been experiencing. You will need determination to land a job with your self-respect intact.

Do We Somehow Hurt Ourselves in the Job Search?

To be aware of what is hindering us, and then to take the necessary steps to change as much as possible, will help us overcome any problems we may be having. If the problem can't be changed, at least we can confront it honestly, acknowledge it, and prepare a statement that we can use when being interviewed. What are some of the things job hunters do whereby they hurt themselves? What factors contribute to poor results in the job search?

As many as 50 percent of all job seekers have a problem with one or more of the following things. None of these things is impossible to overcome. Self-defeating behaviors are not incurable; they can be mastered. Check yourself against this list as a postinterview self-evaluation:

- faulty communication; either talks too little or talks too much; rambles; shows nervousness
- little self-confidence during interview; lacks a positive attitude
- inadequate preparation; failure to ask questions
- inability to respond satisfactorily to questions asked; insufficient knowledge about the company
- late for interview; too casual and breezy; not professional enough
- appearance and mannerisms wouldn't "fit in" with company image
- bad attitude; lots of hidden anger, resentment, and cynicism because of previous job experiences
- psychological/emotional problems detected
- poor written communication
- immature; inflexible; unrealistic expectations
- just generally unqualified for the job
- inability to establish rapport with interviewer; "bad vibes"

Based on how you felt coming out of the interview, would you hire you?

A Word about Reference Checking

Another reason you may have been disqualified from a job could have something to do with the references provided. Did you contact your references and ask permission to use them? If they agreed, did you follow up by sending them a copy of your resume, alerting them that reference-checking calls might be forthcoming? Don't be afraid to ask for a strong endorsement; go over your resume and point out what you did for the company. Reinforce in their minds the positive aspects of your past performance.

If you have reason to believe that a reference is somehow sabotaging your efforts, then you should write, phone, and/ or go see that person if you possibly can.[2] You may have to advise him that his negative input is keeping you from obtaining a new position, making it impossible to support yourself and your family. If this does not result in at least a neutral statement, then you may have to imply that you will seek a legal remedy. Most employers today are aware of the legal consequences of providing a bad reference, and they will tend to cooperate with you.

Overcoming Preconceived Biases

You may be carrying around some preconceived biases and prejudices that you feel others are projecting against you. Sometimes we get stuck in our own trenches. We think others consider us too young/too old; inexperienced/overqualified; too much of a job hopper/too little exposed to the industry; or something else.

Thus we need to do a "reality check." Is any of what you think those interviewing you may be feeling or thinking about you true? Get to work on what might turn out to be obstacles in someone else's thinking, and go in prepared. If you suspect that a question in an interview is related to one of those "obstacles," launch a counteroffensive. Show that you can handle the job. Provide facts, a true "story" from your work experience that substantiates why you applied.

What about That Poor Work History?

For whatever reason, you may have an uneven work performance record. Though your qualifications are ideal and you have made it in for an interview, how are you going to explain short tenure on a job?

The answer is *honestly*. It's not the work history that undermines you, but your difficulty in explaining it. Whatever you do, don't fumble around for answers. Don't get on the defensive and automatically feel that your past is going to work against you. Despite the short tenure, show that you made contributions of lasting value. Go in prepared with good statements and express them with candor and confidence. Show that you can deal with problems, even your own, in a forthright manner. Create the most positive statement(s) you can, and speak well about the job and the people with whom you worked.

Interviewers are searching for strengths you can bring to the job. What is past is prologue, Shakespeare said, and he was right. You need to believe that about yourself and project strength and firm resolve, showcasing your skills, experiences, adaptability, and the fact that you are someone who learned from the past and has grown as a result.

What about Personality Flaws and Other "Impossibilities"?

Do you fear you are being discriminated against because of your size (personal appearance) or personality quirks and flaws? We are not perfect "diamonds," and there may be legitimate things that detract from our marketability.

Nose too big? Who cares? What difference could that possibly make on your job performance? Obese? That could be a liability. Too thin, emaciated looking? What are you doing about it?

Some physical characteristics we can do nothing about: our height, our facial and other bodily features, the way we walk, our speech patterns. Howard Figler recommends focusing on things you can and want to change rather than getting frustrated about the things you can't change. If you are concerned that a prospective employer may judge you inaccurately because of some physical problem, then prepare a statement in advance that you know you can pull out of your repertoire of statements (e.g., "I know I'm small and short and may appear immature for this job, but I assure you I'll present a strong image to the customers and do a good job for you").[3]

Figler points out that unusualness can often be turned to your advantage. "As long as you are comfortable with yourself," he maintains, "you can use your individual features as your calling card." That is, use your "differentness," your peculiar ways or features, as "departure points" for making your life work. Say to yourself, "This is the way I am; this is the way I was created; I am unique, a Designer original," and go forward with confidence.

What about the Competition?

Time after time we encounter the competition in the letters we receive after we have sent in a resume and cover letter or after we have had an interview. Someone "more qualified" or whose skills "more closely matched" what the employer was looking for received the job. This can be very disheartening. I know; I've been there.

What should you do? What did I do? It was back to the drawing board. Figler writes:

> You may very well be faced with a highly competitive field. In that case I advise you to broaden your search in one of several ways: (a) geographically—widen the territory in which you are making contacts; (b) by level—maybe you are shooting too high, try the next level down to see if you can get hired and then promoted; (c) organization—try employers that do similar work, perhaps smaller companies or firms in related areas.
>
> If all this still leads to blank walls, decide what you must do to become competitive in that occupation, set those steps in motion (e.g., formal education, part-time experience, acquisition of skills, volunteer work) and seek an interim job while you are building your case for the longer-range goals. You haven't lost the competition. You're simply going to enter the game at a later date.[4]

Take this excellent advice to heart. I met a number of people for whom this worked. Many older workers find it necessary to acquire word-processing skills. Bookkeepers have to have knowledge of computer spreadsheets to get hired these days. Sales clerks need to know how to punch in billing information. Many people are finding new opportunities in computer-based specialties. Such extra effort doesn't necessarily mean long-term study. A nondegree training program, lasting only a few months, can be an asset. It looks good on your resume to have just completed some current education.

You will have to determine what it is that is creating a job liability for you and then develop a strategy for correcting the situation. While you are doing this, you may need to find a temporary job or get some training. Do whatever it takes to overcome the perceived liability so you can reposition yourself with greater strength.

Are You Undervaluing Yourself?

Sometimes we undervalue ourselves and so disqualify ourselves from potential jobs. Employers are always impressed with individuals who show they have high motivation. An article originating in the *Orlando Sentinel* and picked up by the *Sacramento Bee* (where it caught my attention) by reporter Linda Shrieves says, "Psst! Hey, all you downtrodden, overworked, burned-out flunkies who have been stepped on by a parade of bosses going up the corporate ladder. Got a secret for you! The world cannot be run by bosses alone."

Doesn't that light a fire under you? She's right. "That power-hungry madman really needs peons like us," she says. "Without us, bosses would never get anywhere, never accomplish those year-end goals, never earn that big paycheck. Without us, the boss is nothing."[5]

The American Society for Training and Development (ASTD), a nonprofit professional association representing more than fifty thousand practitioners, managers, administrators, educators, and human resource developers, studied the sixteen skills employers say are basic to success in the workplace. Many of these, such as "self-esteem," are not skills in the traditional sense of the word, but are seen as vital nonetheless.

We are most likely to undervalue ourselves in these kinds of skills: the ability and willingness to learn, oral communication and listening skills, adaptability, problem solving, and creative thinking. Some of the abilities that enable people to acquire jobs and then move up are developmental skills—self-esteem (as mentioned) and motivation/goal setting.

Other highly valued skills include:

- group effectiveness skills—the ability to work with others productively and to develop good interpersonal relationships, teamwork, and negotiation

242

- influencing skills (organization effectiveness and leadership)—allowing people to navigate the sometimes choppy waters in an organization; taking charge and using personal strengths to finish tasks

To project these strengths when being interviewed is crucial. You can do this best by providing examples—true stories or illustrations that are brief, factual, and traceable through your references. Don't sell yourself short by thinking you have the wrong or an inadequate combination of experiences. Remember the word we talked about earlier: *transferable*. Many skills and experiences are transferable into other fields.

Career development is the challenge of reacting to your present circumstances, making the most of what you have, and not settling for less.

What about Educational Handicaps?

What was my job-hunting liability? Many of the positions for which I applied and that I knew I could handle required educational qualifications I didn't possess. Is this your problem? How can you handle it?

The answer is *truthfully*. At no time did I evade the issue. Neither should you. If this is your "problem," you obviously have something going for you, or you couldn't have gotten to the point where you are today. You are an intelligent individual. You have worked hard. It is time for you to start believing your own press. Someone did. You have an interview staring you in the face, or perhaps you have already had that interview.

Here's what I did to make up for a lack of formal education. When the position for which I was applying specifically spelled out the education requirements they wanted, I applied anyway when I knew I was qualified. I deliberately called attention to my educational "shortcomings," violating every "rule" set down in the books. Rather than keeping me from getting an interview, I felt it worked in my favor. I reminded potential employers that I was in good company, supplying information about others like myself.

Many could be cited—individuals who rose to the heights without benefit of a college education, many of them home-schooled. Jim Comstock of Richwood, West Virginia, editor of the weekly *West Virginia Hillbilly* newspaper, has befriended presidents, politicians, and other celebrities through his University of Hard Knocks, called UHK by its alumni. Graduates include U.S. senators Wendell Ford (Kentucky) and Jesse Helms (North Carolina); former U.S. senator Barry Goldwater; former owner of the Oakland A's, Charles O. Finley; Tulsa bank millionaire Lee Braxton; *Washington Times* editor Arnaud de Borchgrave; and Chicago insurance magnate W. Clement Stone.

Famous People Who Didn't Have a College Education

- Peter Jennings, the most popular of the network news anchors (ABC), dropped out of high school in Ottawa, Canada, at age seventeen. Today he earns nearly $2 million.
- Prime Minister John Major left school at age sixteen. He later held the top job in Britain.
- Pearl Buck, the Nobel and Pulitzer Prize–winning novelist, was homeschooled in two countries. The daughter of American missionaries in China, she took Western studies from her mother in the morning and Chinese studies from a tutor in the afternoon.
- Agatha Christie taught herself to read by age five, and her father taught her writing and arithmetic. She attended school briefly, later maintaining that had she

continued her formal education, she would have ended up a "third- or fourth-rate mathematician" rather than a mystery writer.

- Thomas Edison said of his three months of institutional school, "I was always at the foot of the class." When a teacher called the boy "addled," his mother took over his education and taught him a love of learning. Years later the schoolteacher who had insulted the young inventor asked him for financial aid.

- Andrew Wyeth, a world-famous artist, was sickly and educated at home.

"There are a lot of people in the public eye who won't admit they didn't go to college," Comstock says. "They have to be very successful to admit they didn't go to college." Hard Knock graduates are a proud breed. Deservedly so.

I hope you find this encouraging. Many highly educated people are out tramping the streets looking for work, but education alone isn't what gets people jobs. Employers don't hire grades; they hire people. Many successful leaders didn't hit their stride until well after graduation, even with a string of degrees following their name.

You may be someone whose academic record in college was mediocre. (Actually, just completing a course curriculum is a fine accomplishment.) Whether degreed or not, as you build experience and a record of achievements on the job, your education becomes less important. Employers are increasingly concerned with a prospective employee's ability to do the job rather than his or her paper credentials.

To compensate for an educational liability, the need for stressing accomplishments and superior job performance is doubly significant. We need to sell ourselves as cultured, well-informed people. We have to display self-assurance (not arrogance about what we have been able to accomplish) and an abiding belief in our own God-given capabilities.

Interpersonal skills are valued very highly. The *Wall Street Journal* pointed out that many corporate management trainees are "social louts." They may have above average intelligence, "but most lack tact, diplomacy, and understanding of people. Business school graduates are rated especially brash."

I was commended for my achievements when I was called in for interviews and for my honesty in responding to the questions asked about my educational background. Among other things, I told them I supervised persons with degrees and spoke at conferences where highly degreed people made up part of the audience. (Remember what Will Rogers said: "If you done it, it ain't braggin'!")

Be sure to highlight any correspondence courses, seminars, or special training you have received. You may want to look into colleges that offer credit for life accomplishments and go after a degree even now (evenings and/or Saturdays). Retraining and taking course work in specialized fields can be done through part-time studies.

Forrest Sawyer, reporting on an ABC News Special entitled "Revolution at Work," said 85 percent of Americans receive no retraining at all. "If the United States is to stay competitive in the world marketplace, if your children are to have the quality of life you want for them," he said, "we'll all have to become part of a new American revolution."

If you sense your lack of a college degree is a liability in your field of work, getting some training may become a requirement for you even though you have a brilliant record of accomplishments. Only you can make that determination. Generally speaking, though, if you have acquired any worthwhile experience through the years, you will be valued for what you can contribute to a company.

Set yourself apart from the herd and identify what you have accomplished. Don't be afraid to go after the jobs you know you could handle. An education by itself doesn't tell a prospective employer how someone would function on the job. High academic honors and above average grades in college don't always prove someone's worth as a job candidate. More and more, experience is being valued.

There are other common job-hunting liabilities, but just remember, experience is the core of your "sales presentation." In everything you do—from your resume and cover letter to walking through the door into an interview—show a potential employer what you have done and what you are capable of doing. Remember these key words at all times: *abilities, responsibilities, accomplishments.*

> Christ has given each of us special abilities—whatever he wants us to have out of his rich storehouse of gifts.
>
> Ephesians 4:7 TLB

> The Lord is faithful, who will establish you. . . . And we have confidence in the Lord concerning you. . . . Now may the Lord direct your hearts into the love of God and into the patience of Christ.
>
> 2 Thessalonians 3:3–5

Some Final Thoughts

As I come to the end of this book, it is with a strange sort of feeling. As I have written, I have thought of you who are unemployed. Sharing what I have experienced and learned has been like talking to a dear friend. I feel like I am saying good-bye to cherished people. Many have shared their heartaches and experiences with me.

Please know I will continue to care deeply for what happens to you, and I pledge to you my prayerful concern.

> Oh, bless our God. . . .
> For You, O God, have tested us;

You have refined us as silver is refined. . . .
We went through fire and through water;
But You brought us out to rich fulfillment. . . .
Come and hear, all you who fear God,
And I will declare what He has done for my soul.
I cried to Him with my mouth. . . .
Certainly God has heard me;
He has attended to the voice of my prayer.
Blessed be God,
Who has not turned away my prayer,
Nor His mercy from me!

Psalm 66:8, 10, 12, 16–17, 19–20

Don't give up on yourself or God. Continue to do those near-at-hand things that will help to bring order and stability into your life. Then wait patiently for the Lord, trusting him to come to your rescue. Here is a prayer for you to lift to heaven in the days ahead:

Do not withhold Your tender mercies from me, O
    LORD;
Let your lovingkindness and Your truth continually
    preserve me. . . .
Be pleased, O LORD, to deliver me;
O LORD, make haste to help me! . . .
You are my help and my deliverer;
Do not delay, O my God.

Psalm 40:11, 13, 17

Appendix A

Questions and Answers

1. What is unemployment insurance, and how do I go about applying for it?

During the Great Depression, Congress passed legislation that created the Federal-State system of unemployment insurance as a means of providing basic protection for wage earners and for the nation against economic insecurity. The unemployment insurance program was designed to provide survival with dignity for people who become unemployed. It is not a form of charity or relief; nor is eligibility based on economic need. Rather, it is a program designed to help workers, unemployed through no fault of their own, find suitable employment and to pay them benefits while they are seeking employment. You don't have to feel embarrassed or guilty about applying for it. You deserve it and are entitled to it.

However, to be eligible you must:

- have worked for an employer who paid into it (non-profit corporations are exempt)

- be out of work through no fault of your own (if you quit the job without good cause or were discharged for just cause, you disqualify yourself)
- be able to work, be available to work, and be making an effort to secure work (even if it is not in your customary occupation)

You may also file a claim for partial benefits if your steady employer cuts your hours to fewer than a regular full-time week because of a lack of work and you earn less than your unemployment insurance would be if you were completely out of a job. In this event, the employer is required to give you a low-wage notice to take to your local office of the Department of Employment and Training Services.

There is a one-week waiting period after you file your claim before benefits are paid. Once you start receiving benefits, you must report each week to the unemployment office where you first applied. You will not be paid benefits for any week you do not report in. You may ask for and receive permission to mail in your claims. You can expect to receive your first check usually within four weeks from the time of your first visit to the department's office. After that, if you remain out of work and file your claims regularly, your checks should reach you promptly each week in the mail.

Unemployment income is 100 percent taxable with no withholding allowed. However, since your W-2 income will be lower, you may be able to deduct more of your job-hunting expenses. Check with a qualified tax preparer.

In order to be eligible for unemployment insurance, you must be registered for work with the Department of Employment and Training Services and be making an independent search effort. Continuing eligibility is dependent on showing that you are making a sincere effort to find work each week on your own behalf. Keep a record of what you are doing.

2. What is COBRA?

When you become unemployed for whatever reason, and you have been covered under an employer's health and accident plan, you do not have to lose your health insurance. Enacted in 1985, COBRA (the Consolidated Omnibus Budget Reconciliation Act) permits workers to buy coverage under a former employer's health plan for an average of eighteen months after leaving the company. Also covered by COBRA are the employee's spouse and dependents to the extent they were previously covered by the plan. The employer must tell the employee that he or she is entitled to this coverage (sometimes this is not done). Many people are not aware of COBRA. The unemployed person must pay for this insurance, but he or she receives the benefit of the group rate.

COBRA coverage does not apply to employees employed by "small employers" (those employing fewer than twenty employees) or to employees of government agencies or churches.

COBRA coverage ends once a former employee finds a new position with an employer who provides medical coverage (and when that kicks in, usually there is a three-month waiting period) or when he or she becomes eligible for Medicare. Note: If the employee has a preexisting health problem, COBRA will not renew coverage after the eighteen months are over.

3. Where will the jobs be? Where are they now?

The bulk of new jobs are in the field of computer technology and the high-tech field, but that doesn't mean there isn't a place for you in other fields. As shown in this book, medicine and health-related fields are going to provide many job opportunities in the future. The Bureau of Labor Statistics says that ten of the twenty fastest-growing careers are and will be health-related.

As the population ages and sports medicine continues to grow as a specialty, more people will be needed to plan and administer treatment. There will be a great demand for occupational therapists too. Jobs will be in hospitals, nursing homes, and schools. The outlook is good for physical therapists, podiatrists, medical technologists, physician assistants, registered nurses, hospital administrators, dieticians, physicians, cardiologists, ophthalmologists, plastic surgeons, cancer specialists (in great demand), optometrists, and dental hygienists.

Other hot job markets include government workers, legal assistants, systems analysts, employment interviewers, computer programmers, engineers, lawyers, social workers (includes fund-raisers, managers, therapists, and rehabilitation counselors, with many jobs available in clinics, hospitals, nursing homes, and private organizations), accountants, hotel managers (includes a trend to use such people in spas and resorts, inns and motels, cruise ships, and residential apartments).

As stated elsewhere in this book, service-providing industries, including finance, insurance, real estate, government services, and wholesale and retail trade are the largest and fastest-growing major industry group. These jobs will be found in small firms, as well as in large corporations, in all levels of government, and in industries as diverse as banking, data processing, hospitals, and management consulting. The two largest industry groups in this division, health services and business services, are projected to continue to grow very fast, and educational services, which have been growing rapidly, are projected to have average growth.

The service-providing sector jobs conjure up an image of a workforce dominated by cashiers, retail sales workers, and waiters. But that's an inaccurate picture. While the service sector growth will generate millions of clerical, sales, and what we usually think of as service jobs, it will also create jobs for financial managers, engineers, nurses, electrical and electronics technicians, and many other professional and technical workers. This is a broad field with various levels of service involved.

Goods-producing industries are expected to show very little change. This includes construction, manufacturing (actually this will decline), mining, and agriculture (another decline). (These facts were taken from *The Occupational Outlook Handbook* material at www.bls.gov.)

4. What is a "flexible benefits package"?

These are programs offered by employers whereby you can tailor your benefits package by picking and choosing from a "cafeteria style" program. Among the choices: higher disability insurance, a medical plan with varying levels of coverage and deductibles, child care, legal services, extra life insurance. There is a general agreement that a lower salary with substantial benefits can be worth more than a higher salary in terms of its dollar value as a package.

5. What are the odds of succeeding in my own business?

To transition into your own business with little capital is not as easy in today's economic climate as it once was. But to think entrepreneurially is an option that warrants consideration, particularly by certain types of individuals.

What are the odds of succeeding? Statistics say that 65 percent of all new businesses fail within five years. Richard Bolles points out, however, that this means that only about 25 percent of new businesses fail *in any given year*. Year by year, you have a 75 percent chance of succeeding. What this suggests is that *if* you can make it through the first few very difficult years in a new business, your odds of survival increase.

Many of today's most well-known businesses were born out of adversity and job loss. Kentucky Fried Chicken is a good example (hundreds of others could be named). As downsizing and related economic trends wreak their frightening effects on the workplace, more and more individuals begin thinking in terms of entrepreneurship. Many people have a dream in their hearts of starting their own business, and when they find themselves suddenly unemployed, they seek ways to put legs to their dream.

Local Small Business Administration (SBA) centers are a good basic resource, providing pamphlets, counseling, and factual information. In addition, many organizations, such as Minority Business Development Centers, Career Action Centers, and others can be helpful. Research the Internet, the library, and the phone book. At some point you may need the help of an accountant, lawyer, or independent consultant who specializes in developing business plans. If you are going for venture capital, you will need the help of a consultant.

Self-analysis is definitely required. Starting one's own business requires a tenacity and dedication of such intensity that many who do not possess these capabilities will quickly become disillusioned. There are sacrifices to be made, such as trading off time now in relationships with loved ones for future financial rewards. You have to ask yourself questions: Am I prepared for this? Is it going to be worth it? Is my family prepared for this? Will it improve the quality of my life long-term?

Recognize that now, more than ever, there is a high rate of business failures, and the chief reasons for this are undercapitalization, insufficient profits, too much debt, poor growth, inexperience, and heavy operating expenses. I've read that the return on money invested in a business should be at least three times greater than any interest you can earn from a bank. Do you have some "aces in the hole"? That is, do you have a working mate, an inheritance, a pension, savings, a financial backer, a partner, or investors? What assets will you have to put on the line to secure start-up and operating capital?

Conventional wisdom says you can't count on a business producing income for six months. (It may be longer, depending on the nature of the business.) Joyce Lain Kennedy says the entrepreneurship question boils down to a values quiz: What is important to you and what is it worth? What do you have to lose? What do you have to gain? Are you ready to penny pinch for as long as it takes to get your business off the ground and see it thriving?

The old adage about finding a need and filling it still applies. If your business idea can do that, if you are willing to sacrifice and work hard, if you have a clear sense of purpose and clarity in the way you must go to bring your dream to reality, then go for it. While the idea of starting your own business is somewhat scary, many who try it discover that it is one of the best ways to soften the shock of sudden unemployment. As one person said who lost his job and became a successful entrepreneur, "Entrepreneurship suits me fine. I get to control my destiny to a much greater extent than I would in a corporation."

I can speak from experience when discussing starting your own business—the first time was as a young married homemaker when God impressed upon me the need to start a Christian bookstore in the Southern California community where we lived, and the second time many years later as a recently widowed woman in her mid-sixties. Both start-ups succeeded; the first store resulted in a second store also some years later, and I was in the bookstore business for nineteen years. The second venture, a combination antique store, gift shop, and bookstore in a small tourist town in northern California flourished for three-and-a-half years following the death of my husband. I finally closed it when a health problem presented itself; I also felt the need to spend more time in writing. Each entrepreneur experience was a delight; a lot of long hours and hard work, to be sure, but rich learning experiences. What did I learn? Much! I gave each business my all, I was convinced of my "call" to open the stores, I asked God for wisdom and discernment, and I pursued each with a wholehearted dedication to the job at hand. God is a rewarder, and I was rewarded (see Col. 3:23–24).

Below are some home-based business ideas for you to consider that would put you in the classification of being self-employed. They open the door to convenience, flexible hours, and unlimited opportunity yet do not require much investment of up-front monies or involve as much risk.

Sell your services as a consultant or independent contractor. If you know that a gap exists in your particular field, fill it. You may even be able to get your former employer as one of your clients.

Financial analysts point out that there is almost no job— from anesthesiology to zoology—that can't be done on a contract basis. Marketing yourself is one of the hardest parts of doing this—calling cards, brochures, letterheads, and business envelopes will be required. Some cold selling will be necessary as well by telephone and personal calls. Word-of-mouth—friends and people for whom you have done work—will eventually kick in, and if your work is satisfactory, you will be well on your way to success.

You must be able to figure out and set fees for your services and then stick with them. This will take investigation in the marketplace to determine what others in your line of work are charging. Many books with such information are available. A typical consultant's fee breaks down approximately into thirds: one-third covers the cost of the job, another third the nonmarketing overhead, and the final one-third the marketing overhead. Profit added would increase the fee 10 to 20 percent (or more), depending on your particular service. This is a pretty good formula to help you decide what to charge.

Some consultants are thriving and carving out a niche for themselves by helping corporations with training and education programs being farmed out to small specialist firms such as theirs (and/or individuals).

At some point you may want to become part of a professional association; networking will be valuable. You may progress speedily to the point where you will need database information. You may start your own newsletter (desktop publishing would then become a necessity).

Many individuals now market their own newsletters and/or their abilities to write and produce newsletters and brochures for other businesses and organizations locally and nationally. Desktop publishing capabilities have turned where one lives into what is being called "the electronic cottage," whereby an ordinary home becomes a fully functional office thanks to high-tech wizardry.

In fact, the day has arrived when the size and location of one's business is virtually irrelevant. That's good news for the unemployed who have these capabilities and are imaginative and willing to take a plunge.

Consider home party sales as a career option. In today's job market, home party selling offers opportunities for individuals who find themselves suddenly unemployed. It could carry you along through the financial crunch imposed by your job loss while still leaving you free for your job search. You might find, however, that you are so successful at this that it becomes a full-time job. It won't happen overnight, but some earn $50,000 to $100,000 per year and more.

Three things in particular are required: persistence, belief in yourself, and a love of people, according to veterans of Tupperware, Mary Kay Cosmetics, Princess House Crystal, and Home Interiors and Gifts, to name just a few. These companies (and others) offer product lines that are well-known and respected worldwide. And they offer lucrative career opportunities with flexible hours as well. Many homemakers moonlight in this way, bringing in needed financial help while still raising a family. I know many successful women who do this.

No previous training is required. All companies provide training and lots of moral support at no cost. The initial expenditure generally requires investing in a display case or assortment of products (which is not an exorbitant investment). Look in your telephone directory for information if this sounds like something you could do. Use the Internet.

Home-based businesses are booming! No one knows exactly how many home-based businesses there are, but virtually all research experts agree that the number of home-based entrepreneurs will increase in the coming years.

Whatever the home-based business or consulting service you offer, these rules apply (just as they do in any other business): research your idea, write a business plan, accumulate some start-up capital, and prepare a marketing strategy. This is the foundation upon which you can build your own work future.

Could you go on the speaking circuit? Are you a good speaker? Do you think well on your feet? Professional organizations are always searching for gifted speakers and/or entertainers.

These are just some ideas to trigger your imagination. Go for it!

6. Is there a "secret to success"?

Robert Half International, Inc., surveyed vice presidents and personnel directors and asked them to choose the single most important element necessary for a successful career. Here's the tally:

- hard work: 52 percent
- intelligence: 21 percent

- experience: 9 percent
- personality: 6 percent

For a Christian, success is finding God's will and doing it. That may sound simplistic, but it is true. Combine that with the above ingredients and you have a winning combination. Dietrich Bonhoeffer wrote in *Letters and Papers from Prison* that to keep in step with eternity, we must remember that everything has its time. The main thing is that we keep step with God and do not keep pressing on a few steps ahead nor keep dawdling a step behind.

7. What does the "hidden job market" mean?

Eighty percent of jobs are found not through formal sources like newspaper advertising, but through the "hidden job market" that comes from word of mouth. Husbands and wives tell everyone they know that their mate is looking for work; friends broadcast this information for their friends; family members tell other family members. Actually, it is networking carried to its broadest means.

The "hidden job market" is something of a misnomer. Actually, the job isn't hidden as much as it is just not public knowledge. Often it comes and goes before most people know there is even a vacancy within an organization. That is why networking is so important. The challenge is to find those contacts within those markets where you would like to become employed and tap into them as a primary source. They must be individuals who are willing to become true sources of information.

Here are some possibilities you may be overlooking:

- Business cards. After I was reemployed, one day I came across a business card file with probably a hundred or so cards, and I realized I hadn't once consulted this valuable potential resource.

- Executives for whom you worked in the past
- Co-workers with whom you worked in the past
- Professional acquaintances: a neighbor who is a stockbroker, a doctor, a lawyer, your banker or accountant; real estate agents and brokers; elected officials whom you know personally; salespeople, etc.
- Members of clubs or associations to which you belong
- Affluent friends
- Your church family
- Your local Chamber of Commerce; city hall
- Your mailing list (e.g., Christmas card list)
- Your checkbook (Go through old checks. You might be surprised at a name or business you are overlooking.)
- The telephone book, especially by categories in the Yellow Pages

Be discreet when contacting those people who would be considered as hidden job market lead possibilities. Restrain yourself from coming on too strong. Be tactful. Ethical. Courteous.

8. What is the church doing for the unemployed?

Churches and religious groups are rallying around the unemployed and have been doing so now for years. Hopefully, this book and ongoing media reports on the plight of the unemployed will direct the church's attention to the need to put legs to their prayers for the jobless.

Many churches are providing workshops and resources. Check the churches in your own area; watch your local newspapers. Locally, where I reside in the greater Dallas metroplex, I see news stories with headlines such as "Job Hunting Is Serious Business and Ministry" and "Local Church Offers Free Career Forums: Obtaining an Interview in a Tight Job Market." These Flower Mound, Texas, churches are on the cutting edge of providing help that the unemployed in not only their churches but the community so desperately need.[1] Putting biblical principles to work in the marketplace of ideas and potentiality is an idea whose time has more than come.

The *Dallas Morning News* carried a story highlighting the efforts of the Northwest Bible Church, whose organizers offer job-hunting guidance based on biblical principles. "Unfortunately, it's one of the fastest-growing ministries in town," the story revealed. The curriculum offered is called "Career Transition Workshop," which has become a proven model of a "faith walk in addition to a job search," according to Bill Micale, one of the individuals who has spearheaded the workshops in San Antonio and other Texas cities and even nationwide. Similar programs are offered in other churches.

Appendix B

Recommended Reading

There are far more books available that will aid you in your job search than I can possibly mention here. Browse through bookstores and the library; make notes and do comparison shopping. If you use the services of a job counselor, he or she will probably recommend books to read or loan you books. Always read with a notepad in hand, and write down information you can apply in your job search.

If you plan to buy resources off the Internet, factor in the shipping and handling charges for any books or material you order.

Books Referred to in This Book

Richard Nelson Bolles, the latest *What Color Is Your Parachute?* (Ten Speed Press), and/or any of his older books. Published annually with new information added each year; a resource of incalculable value. Paper and pencil exercises will help you identify what kind of work climate you will flourish in. Worksheets scattered throughout the book help you prioritize your skills, etc. A very valuable resource.

Kenneth M. and Sheryl N. Dawson, *Job Search: The Total System* (John Wiley & Sons). Techniques to aid you in mastering the major elements of a job search. Material that will help make you "market fit."

Judith A. Dubin and Melanie R. Keveles, *Fired for Success* (Warner Books). Full of practical, easy-to-read material that will help you turn the loss of your job into an opportunity.

Howard Figler, *The Complete Job-Search Handbook: All the Skills You Need to Get Any Job and Have a Good Time Doing It* (Henry Holt). A very important book; one I referred to over and over again.

Robert Half, *How to Get a Better Job in This Crazy World* (Crown). By the founder of Robert Half International and Accountemps, a man who started recruiting job seekers forty years ago. A wealth of experience to draw upon arranged for easy reference.

Joyce Lain Kennedy. This nationally syndicated columnist has a twice-weekly "Careers" column appearing in more than a hundred newspapers. Here are four books you might want to look at: *Hook Up, Get Hired!*, *The Internet Job Search Handbook* (coauthor), *Electronic Job Search Revolution*, and *Electronic Resume Revolution*, all published by John Wiley & Sons.

Kathryn and Ross Petras, *The Only Job Hunting Guide You'll Ever Need* (Poseidon Press). A comprehensive guide providing definitive step-by-step approaches to take you through a job search. Nicely formatted, making it easy to follow. Full of ingenious ideas and techniques.

Some of these books may no longer be available, or they may have been revised and updated with new titles. Look for them on the Internet by author first. These were the materials that proved valuable to me while I was searching for a position, and I worked diligently to assimilate the information they contained into my thinking in order to save you much time and money. As I worked on the new edition of this book, this material was as up-to-date and as relevant today as it was when I wrote the first edition.

Books to Help in Becoming a Consultant

Howard L. Shenson, *Shenson on Consulting* and/or *The Contract and Fee-Setting Guide for Consultants and Professionals* (John Wiley & Sons). The best books I found for providing information on contracting and fee setting that would be both profitable for you and equitable for your clients. Detailed, research-based strategies to help you effectively build and maintain a consulting practice. The author is called the "Consultant's Consultant."

Books for Entrepreneurs

Books for entrepreneurs abound, and you are well advised to research and choose carefully. Success stories of those who launched their own businesses and empires can be very motivating. Rather than sit in front of the computer for hours on end, invest that time in some reading that will enrich your thinking and spur you to action. "Reading maketh a full man" is a truism worth thinking about. Gas tanks don't run on empty; neither do minds.

Books on Foundations Offering Grant Money and Information on Government Money

Information on grants and government money can be found on the Internet, but often a subscription fee is charged by the services providing the information. Consult with your librarian or even your banker for information on funding possibilities. Beyond that, here are some directories you may find in your library:

The Foundation Directory, furnished by The Foundation Center, 79 Fifth Ave., New York, NY 10003. An alphabetical state-by-state directory and reference guide for private and community U.S. grant-making foundations that held assets of $1 million or more or gave $100,000 or more in the last year of record.

Matthew Lesko, *Getting Yours: The Complete Guide to Government Money* (Viking Penguin).

I haven't begun to scratch the surface on books and reading material that will expand your pool of information. Richard Bolles does the most thorough job of this of any books I have consulted. His book(s) will readily be found in any library. Beyond this, ask a reference librarian at your library for help, spelling out specifically what you are seeking.

Appendix C

A Guide to Library Research

The range of information available through library research is mind-boggling, but don't let it overwhelm you. There are three main sources of information you should probe: *reference directories*, *trade publications*, and *newspapers*. These materials are not available for checkout.

You can also boil down your research to three areas: *an occupational field* (or fields of your choice), *specific organizations* (within that field or fields), and *specific people* (background data on individuals who make hiring decisions). The information found in reference directories, trade publications, and newspapers can be funneled into these categories.

A loose-leaf notebook works well to record this information. Sometimes you may want to copy articles and insert them in the appropriate sections.

Business Journals, Newspapers, Specific Trade Publications

You will want to follow ads in area papers, the *National Business Employment Weekly* (published by the *Wall Street Journal*), other major city newspapers, and trade and professional journals. General business magazines, such as *Forbes*, *Fortune*, *Inc.*, *Barron's*, and *Business Week* should also be followed. Read not only for job leads, but for the information they can reveal to you about what is happening in the job market and, in particular, your field.

You may decide to subscribe to some of these papers and journals or make weekly trips to the library.

Few things will be of more help to you than the trade-specific publications that every industry publishes. These provide an insider's view of the field you have targeted. Look for them in the business periodicals section at the library.

Trade Journals Information

Standard Periodical Directory
Standard Rate & Data Service Business Publications

Stock Reports and Annual Reports

Standard & Poor's Stock Reports
The Value Line Investment Survey

Read the annual reports of individual companies (call the company and request this information if you can't find it in the library). 10-K reports are on file with the SEC for all public corporations. If you are in an executive position, it would be worth your while to acquaint yourself with this information. *Value Line* will give you a good "feel" for a company, its management style, and so on.

For information on specific industries, inform the librarian, and he or she will show you what to look for and what specialized journals and directories will be useful.

Periodical Indexes Information

Business Periodicals Index
Predicasts F&S Index United States
Wall Street Journal Index
Indexes on other major papers should be available as well.

For the most part, information older than six months will serve no useful purpose unless it is a major news story and you need it to relate intelligently to the company in your cover letter.

Local and Regional Newspapers Information

Ayers Directory of Publications
Gale Directory of Publications (indexed geographically to enable you to find information on a newspaper or magazine that covers a particular area of the United States)

Reference Directories

These directories will enable you to find the most basic information you need, having a wealth of information. Glean carefully.

Directories in Print (Gale Research Company). Information can be used to find industry-specific directories that would be helpful in targeting resumes.

The Directory of Directories (2 vols.). Information on almost any field or subject.

The Dun & Bradstreet Business Rankings. Public and private businesses ranked within informational sections, by company alphabetically, by sales and employee size, within state and within industry category by sales volume and employee size.

Dun & Bradstreet Reference Book of Corporate Managements (Dun & Bradstreet). Profiles of top corporate managers including addresses, phone numbers, education, employment history, etc. Also lists biographies of vice presidents who often are the people who do the interviewing.

Dun's Million Dollar Directory (multivolumes). Lists U.S. businesses in a variety of industries. Alphabetical, geographic, and industry classifications.

The Encyclopedia of Associations (3 vols.) (Gale Research Company). Lists trade and professional associations.

Encyclopedia of Business Information Sources (Gale Research Company). A one-volume resource designed to provide a means for quickly scanning many of the sources that exist on more than 1,100 business-related topics.

Moody's Industrial Manual (Moody's Investor Service, Inc.).

Standard & Poor's Register of Corporations, Directors and Executives (Standard & Poor's Corporation).

Standard & Poor's Register of Corporations, Directors and Executives (Vol. 2) (Standard & Poor's). Biographies of executives and directors with addresses, etc.

Thomas Register (12 vols.) (Thomas Publishing Company).

Consultants and Executive Recruiters Information

Association of Executive Search Consultants (AESC).

Consultants and Consulting Organizations Directory (Gale Research Company). Lists firms, individuals, and organizations engaged in career consulting work.

Directory of Executive Recruiters (Kennedy & Kennedy, Inc.).

Executive Employment Guide (American Management Assn.).

Yellow Pages provide helpful information on business and industry in a particular location that may be of interest to you.

Use these library resources, especially magazines, journals, and newspapers creatively as a way to stimulate your thinking about options that might not otherwise occur to you.

This is by no means a comprehensive list of the vast collections of material that will be helpful to you in job hunting. The information is virtually limitless. What I have attempted to do is provide a summary to whet your appetite and move you in the right direction.

Notes

Introduction

1. Stephen Covey, *The Seven Habits of Highly Effective People* (New York: Simon and Schuster, 1989), 71, 73, 75, 86.

Chapter 1: When the Unthinkable Happens to You

1. Richard Bolles, *What Color Is Your Parachute?* 1991 ed. (Berkeley, CA: Ten Speed Press, 1991), 46.

2. These figures are according to the *World Competitiveness Report 1990*, compiled by the International Institute for Management Development and the World Economic Forum, both in Switzerland.

3. Christina Wise, "Temp Staffing Ticks Up as Cautious Employers See Demand Building," *Investor's Business Daily*, October 23, 2003, 1.

4. Angela Shah, "Consumers Sing No-Jobs Blues," *Dallas Morning News*, June 14, 2003.

5. Joyce Lain Kennedy, "Long job search could use refueling," *Dallas Morning News*, March 16, 2003.

6. Jack Nehlig, "Off-Shore Moves Hurt, Help," *DESIGN NEWS*, September 22, 2003.

7. Ron Wilson, "Outsource Tide Won't Ebb," *Electronic Engineering Times*, September 29, 2003, http://www.eetimes.com/showArticle.jhtml?articleID=183 09247.

8. Ibid.

9. Ibid.

10. Ibid., 57.

11. Alvin Toffler, *Powershift* (New York: Bantam Books, 1990).

12. J. B. Phillips, *New Testament Christianity* (London: Hodder and Stoughton, 1936), 70, 72.

Chapter 2: The First Things to Do (or Consider Doing)

1. Peter Drucker, paraphrased in Covey, *Seven Habits*, 154.

2. E. M. Gray, "The Common Denominator of Success," cited by Covey, *Seven Habits*, 148–49.

3. Christina Wise, "Temp Staffing Ticks Up as Cautious Employers See Demand Building," *Investor's Business Daily*, October 23, 2003, 11.

4. Ibid.

Chapter 3: Private Victories Precede Public Victories

1. Charles Hembree, *Pocket of Pebbles* (Grand Rapids: Baker, 1969), 36.

2. Covey, *Seven Habits*, 40, 60.

3. Arthur Gordon, *A Touch of Wonder* (Old Tappan, NJ: Revell, 1974), 73.

4. Covey, *Seven Habits*, 24.

5. David Knuth, "Diary of an Unemployed EE: Fending Off Despair Half the Battle," *Electronic Engineering News*, September 29, 2003, 30.

Chapter 4: Be a Master, Not a Victim, of Your Situation

1. Perhaps you will take exception to that statement. You may be thinking about 1 John 3:17–18, where we are told to minister to one another's needs. John says that if we have this world's goods and see a brother in need yet shut up our hearts from him, it's questionable that the love of God abides in us. John adds, "My little children, let us not love in word or in tongue, but in deed and in truth" (v. 18). You may be thinking of Jesus's words in Matthew's Gospel, where he speaks of those who are in great need (hungry, thirsty, in need of clothing, sick, or in prison) and the necessity of meeting those needs (see Matt. 25:31–46). This is set in the context of future judgment, and those who fail to respond are told, "When you refused to help the least of these my brothers, you were refusing to help me" (v. 45 TLB). I've observed that people sometimes fall short of biblical standards. This is no excuse, of course, but it is reality.

Chapter 5: Where Do You Go from Here?

1. Emily Koltnow and Lynne S. Dumas, *Congratulations! You've Been Fired* (New York: Fawcett Columbine, 1990).

2. Everyone needs a Barbara Johnson in his or her life. If you can't know her personally, the next best thing is to read her books. Some of them are: *Where Does a Mother Go to Resign?*, *Fresh Elastic for Stretched-Out Moms*, *Stick a Geranium in Your Hat and Be Happy*, *Plant a Geranium in Your Cranium*, *Splashes of Joy in the Cesspools of Life*, *God's Most Precious Jewels Are Crystallized Tears*, *Pack*

Up Your Gloomies in a Great Big Box, Living Somewhere Between Estrogen and Death, He's Gonna Toot and I'm Gonna Scoot, Leaking Laffs between Pampers and Depends, I'm So Glad You Asked Me What I Didn't Wanna Hear. The titles give you some indication of her humor and insightfulness.

3. Howard D. Figler, *The Complete Job-Search Handbook* (New York: Henry Holt, 1988).

4. Joyce Lain Kennedy, "Go high-touch instead of high-tech," *Dallas Morning News,* April 27, 2003.

5. Kennedy, "Long job search could use refueling," *Dallas Morning News,* March 16, 2003.

Chapter 6: Chasing the Pink-Slip Blues

1. Judith A. Dubin and Melanie R. Keveles, *Fired for Success: How to Turn Losing Your Job into the Opportunity of a Lifetime* (New York: Warner Books, 1990), 10.

2. Elisabeth Kübler-Ross, *On Death and Dying* (New York: Macmillan, 1970), chaps. 1–7.

3. Lee Iacocca with William Novak, *Iacocca: An Autobiography* (New York: Bantam Books, 1984), prologue.

4. Dubin and Keveles, *Fired,* 10.

5. Reported by Daniel Q. Haney, Associated Press science writer. "It is the first evidence for an association between stress and a biologically verifiable infectious disease," said the study's director, Dr. Sheldon Cohen of Carnegie Mellon University in Pittsburgh. Dr. Janice Kiecolt-Glaser of Ohio State University said, "It is one of the very best pieces of work ever conducted in this area." Date unknown.

6. *Take Charge of Your Health* by Gladys Lindberg and Judy Lindberg McFarland (Harper & Row) is the book I had the privilege of assisting in writing. Recently updated, it is now called *Aging without Growing Old.*

7. Dubin and Keveles, *Fired.*

Chapter 7: The Age Factor

1. Quoted in "On the Job: Trends in the Workplace; Should You Take the Job Buyout Offer?" *The San Francisco Sunday Examiner & Chronicle,* February 10, 1991.

2. Ibid.

3. Kennedy, "Work to keep fire in the belly," *The Dallas Morning News,* April 6, 2003.

Chapter 8: Turning the Corner

1. Harvey Mackay, *Swim with the Sharks without Being Eaten Alive* (New York: William Morrow, 1988), 191.

2. As quoted by Phyllis Schneider in "Career Charisma," *Working Woman,* May 1988, 80.

3. Quoted in Lloyd C. Douglas, *The Big Fisherman* (New York: Houghton Mifflin, 1952, 1976).

Chapter 9: The Market-Driven Approach

1. Mackay, *Swim with the Sharks*, 230.
2. Figler, *Complete Job-Search Handbook*, 68.
3. Ibid., 281.
4. Ibid., 197.
5. Ibid., 202.
6. Ibid., 281.
7. Ibid.

Chapter 10: Resumania

1. Robert Half, *How to Get a Better Job in This Crazy World* (New York: Crown, 1990).
2. Bolles, *What Color Is Your Parachute?* 2002 ed. (Berkeley, CA: Ten Speed Press, 2002), chapter 3, especially 33–35.
3. Kennedy, "Job referral bonus may pay off," *Dallas Morning News*, September 21, 2003.
4. Kenneth M. Dawson and Sheryl N. Dawson, *Job Search: The Total System* (New York: John Wiley & Sons, 1988), 55.

Chapter 11: Writing to Influence

1. William Zinsser, *On Writing Well* (New York: Harper & Row, 1989), 9.
2. Kathryn Petras and Ross Petras, *The Only Job Hunting Guide You'll Ever Need* (New York: Poseidon, 1999), 174.
3. Zinsser, *On Writing Well*, 26.
4. Deborah Dumaine, *Write to the Top: Writing for Corporate Success* (New York: Random House, 1989), 91.
5. Zinsser, *On Writing Well*, 25.
6. Ibid., 39.
7. Ibid., 9.
8. Dawson and Dawson, *Job Search*, 55.

Chapter 12: The Job Interview

1. Mackay, *Swim with the Sharks*, 196.
2. Iacocca, *Iacocca*.
3. Dawson and Dawson, *Job Search*.
4. Petras and Petras, *The Only Job Hunting Guide*, 193.
5. Figler, *Complete Job-Search Handbook*, 199–200.
6. Adapted from Dubin and Keveles, *Fired for Success*, 36–37.

7. Lewis R. Elin, president of Topps Manufacturing Co., Rochester, IN, quoted in "A Little Advice from an Interviewer," *South Bend Tribune*.

8. Petras and Petras, *The Only Job Hunting Guide*, 198–203.

Chapter 13: The Job Offer

1. Joyce Lain Kennedy, "Pay Negotiation Is Crucial Skill," *Dallas Morning News*, March 23, 2003, jobcenter.dallasnews.com.

2. Figler, *Complete Job-Search Handbook*.

3. Dawson and Dawson, *Job Search*, 150.

Chapter 14: When You Don't Get the Job Offer

1. A. W. Tozer, *The Root of the Righteous* (Camp Hill, PA: Christian Publications, 1986), 12–13.

2. J. B. Phillips, *Your God Is Too Small* (New York: Macmillan, 1961), 49.

3. Tozer, *Root of the Righteous*, 50–51.

4. Philip Yancey, *Disappointment with God* (Grand Rapids: Zondervan, 1988), 186.

Chapter 15: Final Considerations

1. Erwin R. Lutzer, *Failure: The Back Door to Success* (Chicago: Moody Press, 1975), 127.

2. This is a very biblical approach, according to Matthew 5:21–25. God's laws are meant as a hedge of protection around our lives. So if loss of your job left you with an unsettled account at your last place of employment, clear it up. Do what has to be done so that you are not hindered in your job search.

3. I am indebted to Howard Figler's book *The Complete Job-Search Handbook* for insights gleaned for this material.

4. Figler, *Complete Job-Search Handbook*, 283.

5. Linda Shrieves, "Learning His or Her Goals Is Key to 'Managing' Boss," *Sacramento Bee*, December 30, 1990. Originally reported in the *Orlando Sentinel*.

Appendix A

1. Mary A. Jacobs, "Putting biblical principles to work," *Dallas Morning News*, March 23, 2003, 2G. "Local Church Offers Free Career Forums," *Messenger*, Flower Mound, Texas, February 6, 2004, 21. Pamela A. King, "Job Hunting Is Serious Business and Ministry," *News Connection*, Flower Mound, Texas, January 30–February 13, 2004, 10.

Index

Helen Kooiman Hosier is well known in the field of Christian communications both as a writer and as a speaker. This bookstore owner turned author has more than sixty titles to her credit, including *Living the Lois Legacy: Passing on a Lasting Faith to Your Grandchildren*; *100 Christian Women Who Changed the Twentieth Century*; *Beyond the Norm*; *Jonathan Edwards: The Great Awakener*; *William and Catherine Booth: Founders of the Salvation Army*; *Footprints: The True Story Behind the Poem*; *Living Cameos*; *Cameos: Women Fashioned by God*; and others. She conveys biblical principles with conviction and depth of understanding born out of her life experiences. She lives in Flower Mound, Texas.